"In the spirit of Minsky and Kindleberger, Tokunaga offers an original account of dollar dominance, highlighting its dynamic and crisis-prone nature. He locates its core in endogenous, collateral-driven shadow banking and balance-sheet dynamics, with United States Treasury securities serving as universal collateral. This distinctive agenda goes beyond available accounts. A must-read!"

Hasan Cömert, *Associate Professor of Economics at Trinity College, CT, USA*

"How has the dollar survived at the top of the international currency pyramid through decades of global financial turmoil? Is it destined to remain at the top indefinitely? Junji Tokunaga's *Dollar Dominance: Fundamentals, Nature, and Present Structure* addresses these important questions with careful, painstaking, and extremely clear analyses of the recent history and underlying structures of the international financial markets and their relationship with the US dollar. The book is remarkable in that it tackles enormously complex issues—such as the underlying 'plumbing' of various financial markets—with great clarity and ease of exposition. I hope all my students read this excellent book. I know I will assign it to them."

Gerald Epstein, *Professor of Economics and Co-Director of Political Economy Research Institute (PERI), University of Massachusetts Amherst, USA*

"This book unravels an enigma as follows: What supports the US dollar hegemony in the last few decades of financialization in which all kinds of wealth present itself as 'an immense amount of fictitious capital'?"

Takuyoshi Takada, *Emeritus Professor at Chuo University, Tokyo, Japan*

Dollar Dominance

This book critically analyzes the US dollar's dominance as an international currency through an analysis of US dollar gross balance sheets in the shadow banking system at global, systematically important banks.

It begins by drawing upon Minsky and Kindleberger's financial fragility hypothesis, explaining how analysis of dynamics in balance sheet expansion helps to reveal the fundamentals of the dollar standard system. It then examines the dollar standard system in the 2000s and during the Global Financial Crisis (GFC) of 2007–09, showing how endogenous finance of the dollar drove said banks to overstretch their balance sheets. An analysis of the dollar standard system post-crisis suggests that US Treasury securities as universal collateral assets have acted as a bedrock for the present dollar standard system.

Dollar Dominance will interest scholars and graduate students of international finance, monetary systems, money, and banking. It is also a useful resource for central bankers, financial regulators, and other finance industry professionals.

Junji Tokunaga is a Professor at the Department of Economics, Dokkyo University, Saitama, Japan. His research focuses on the international monetary system.

Routledge Focus on Economics and Finance

The fields of economics are constantly expanding and evolving. This growth presents challenges for readers trying to keep up with the latest important insights. Routledge Focus on Economics and Finance presents short books on the latest big topics, linking in with the most cutting-edge economics research.

Individually, each title in the series provides coverage of a key academic topic, whilst collectively the series forms a comprehensive collection across the whole spectrum of economics.

Corporate Short-Term Financing in Europe
The Role of Trade Credit and Bank Loans in Liquidity Management
Julia Koralun-Bereźnicka

Financial Resilience and the Sustainable Development Goals
Edited by Magdalena Ziolo and Bruno S. Sergi

Geopolitics, China, and the Global Supply Chain
Issues and Implications
Sarah Chan

Proactivity in Economics
Between Resourcefulness and Entrepreneurship
Jakub Bożydar Wiśniewski

The Geoeconomics of Global Value Chains
Navigating Geopolitical Complexity and Industrial Policy Shifts
Katarzyna Mroczek-Dąbrowska

Dollar Dominance
Fundamentals, Nature, and Present Structure
Junji Tokunaga

For more information about this series, please visit: www.routledge.com/Routledge-Focus-on-Economics-and-Finance/book-series/RFEF

Dollar Dominance

Fundamentals, Nature, and Present Structure

Junji Tokunaga

Routledge
Taylor & Francis Group
LONDON AND NEW YORK

First published 2026
by Routledge
4 Park Square, Milton Park, Abingdon, Oxon OX14 4RN

and by Routledge
605 Third Avenue, New York, NY 10158

Routledge is an imprint of the Taylor & Francis Group, an informa business

British Library Cataloguing-in-Publication Data
A catalogue record for this book is available from the British Library

ISBN: 9781041227878 (hbk)
ISBN: 9781041227885 (pbk)
ISBN: 9781003733959 (ebk)

DOI: 10.4324/9781003733959

Typeset in Times New Roman
by codeMantra

Contents

Foreword

by **Gerald Epstein**
Professor of Economics and Co-Director of Political Economy Research Institute (PERI)
University of Massachusetts Amherst
USA
October 16, 2025

For more than 20 years, domestic and international financial markets have been in periodic upheaval and turbulent change. The Great Financial Crisis of 2007–08 almost brought the world economy to its knees, the euro crisis soon followed, with the COVID crisis right behind which itself almost caused a generalized financial meltdown. Soon thereafter, in 2023, we witnessed the collapse of Silicon Valley Bank, and Credit Suisse, and near breakdown of Signature Bank, and First Republic. The structure of financial markets evolved dramatically during these major events, with the meteoric rise of non-bank financial institutions and growth of asset management companies, and the mysterious rise of the so-called "shadow" financial sector.

But despite these momentous changes, at least one financial pillar stayed firmly in place: the international role of the US dollar. Despite blips and fluctuations, the dollar has remained supreme, relative to other national "hard" currencies such as the euro, Swiss franc, Japanese yen, and Chinese renminbi. This supremacy holds with respect to the major international roles of currencies: as central bank reserves, anchor currency against which countries stabilize their currencies, units of account by which countries price key products such as oil, and means of payment by which countries denominate and pay their international debts.

This remarkable stability in the face of so much turmoil cries out for answers to numerous burning questions: How has the dollar's role been able to withstand such massive financial changes? Was this resilience simply a market phenomenon or was it also promoted by government policies? What has been the impact of this continuing central role for the dollar? Has it helped to stabilize the global financial system, or has it itself been one of the factors leading to financial turmoil? And, finally: Is the "past prologue"? Will this resilience of the dollar continue long into the future? This question has become especially burning in the current moment when the Trump administration in the United States has upended the geopolitical system with tariffs, attacks on the independence of the Federal Reserve, and other domestic and international actions that have led some to believe that the post-World War II order, which ushered in Pax Americana and the international role of the dollar, is now on the way out.

Junji Tokunaga's *Dollar Dominance: Fundamentals, Nature, and Present Structure* addresses these important questions with careful, painstaking, and extremely clear analyses of the recent history and underlying structures of the international financial markets and their relationship with the US dollar. The book is remarkable in that it tackles some enormously complex issues—such as the underlying "plumbing" of various financial markets such as collateral trading, repos and reverse repos, and the like, but it does so with great clarity and ease of exposition. Given Tokunaga's vast number of references and careful documentation, it appears that he has read almost everything on these topics and utilized these resources not to bury the reader in a blizzard of detail, but to edify her.

In doing so, Tokunaga not only describes and explains the rise and fall of the international financial markets in the course of various booms, busts, and financial crises, but he never loses sight of the key questions: how has the dollar survived through all of this, why has it remained at the top of the currency pyramid, what impact has it had on the nature and stability of the global financial system, and is it destined to remain at the top indefinitely?

Tokunaga places at the center of the analysis the comparative advantage of the US dollar relative to its main rival, the euro, in facilitating financial operations in the offshore and shadow markets, in a world where "safe assets" and collateralized financial transactions are central to global financial transactions. This is a world that is very, very far from the traditional, pristine visions of international finance common in textbooks: the role of international finance is to facilitate international trade and investment, and to help savers acquire wealth portfolios that perfectly trade off risk and return. In fact, shows Tokunaga, the international financial markets have become enormous self-referential financial loops for betting, speculating, and trading which, only occasionally, directly connect with the underlying fundamentals of trading, insuring, saving, and investing.

He shows that the dollar's advantage over the euro depends on several factors—which Tokunaga well explains: the military prowess of the US, the role of the Federal Reserve as lender of last resort, and the crucial role US Treasury securities play as "safe assets" to be used as collateral and safe haven investments. These, denominated as they are in the US dollar, dominate

Europe and the euro where the legal structure does not facilitate either an effective lender of last resort or the issuance of European wide debt that can be used as safe assets for these purposes.

Tokunaga shows how these characteristics supported the continued role of the dollar, but also how the role of the dollar facilitated financial crises, especially the Great Financial Crisis of 2007–08. By drawing finance from Europe into the subprime real estate lending markets and exotic financial products like collateralized debt obligations (CDOs) and credit default swaps (CDS)—short-term lending that could flee at the drop of a rumor—the dollar-based system helped to create a dollar-based crisis. When this crisis hit, the Federal Reserve led a dollar-based bailout. This bailout not only supported myriad financial institutions, markets, and actors, but also saved the dollar itself.

Should we infer from all these arguments that the dominant dollar is here to stay for the foreseeable future?

Tokunaga gives a thoughtful and nuanced answer to this question. At a time when many are predicting the end of the dollar system, while others are claiming that the dollar is invincible, Tokunaga convincingly argues that, while the dollar still has many advantages over its closest rival, the euro, it is still quite vulnerable. Its vulnerability stems mainly from the fact that it facilitates financial crises and requires bailouts from the Federal Reserve. If the crises get worse, as some predict will likely happen because of the rise of crypto, stable coins, and financial deregulation more generally pushed by the US, then the economic and political viability of continuing Federal Reserve bailouts might be called into question. If this happens, then the dollars dominance might be at risk.

Tokunaga does not give a definitive answer to this question. But he arms the rest of us with the information and tools we need to delve further and come up with our own assessments of this and other important questions about our current international financial system and the dollar's role. I hope all my students read this excellent book. And I hope yours do, too.

Preface

We have been living in the world of the US dollar-centric international monetary system since World War II (WWII). The Bretton Woods (BW) system signed in 1944 envisioned a gold-dollar standard system that would stabilize the dollar-centric international monetary system after WWII. The US' unilateral closing of the gold window, called 'Nixon Shock', in August 1971 brought an end to the gold-dollar standard system, precipitating a nonsystem. Still, the emergence of a nonsystem was not the end of the dollar-centric international monetary system but marked the transition to the US dollar standard system in 1973.

Since the Global Financial Crisis (GFC) of 2007–09, there has been increasing discussion on why the dollar standard system has been maintained in the post-BW system era. Among other things, the money view, which has become increasingly common in heterodox academics, provides a systematic analysis of the dollar standard that has three distinguishing features. First, the dollar standard system can be taken for granted, in the sense that the contemporary international monetary system is inherently viewed as an international currency hierarchy where the dollar has been at the top and all other major currencies have been pushed down to peripheral positions. Second, the intuitional development in the hierarchical structure of the global dollar supply allows the dollar standard to have 'systemic nature', despite no defined and agreed official frameworks for stabilizing the dollar-centric international monetary system in the post-BW system period. And last, evolution of the US Federal Reserve (Fed) as an international lender of last resort (LLR) since the GFC contributes to the 'status quo' dollar standard system where the dollar is dominant in the 2010s.

However, what has emerged as the dollar standard cannot be regarded as an 'invincible' system. First, it is incorrect that the US dollar's staying power has always been unrivaled. The dollar's dominance has, gradually but distinctly, been undermined by the internationalization of the German Deutsche mark and Japanese yen since the second half of the 1980s, and then the rising role of the euro in the 2000s. The emergence of the euro was the first time since the collapse of the BW system that the US dollar standard system faced real currency competition in the 2000s. Second, the dollar standard system has essentially entailed global financial instability. Looking historically at the dollar standard system since the 1970s, we can see that unfettered global capital flows triggered the recurrence of an international currency and monetary crisis that climaxed as the GFC of 2007–09, which had its very epicenter in the US. Finally, the extraordinary sell-off in the US Treasury markets as the largest, deepest, and most liquid financial markets in the world, at the height of the COVID-19 financial meltdown in March 2020, led to unprecedented pressure on global dollar funding, which would have destabilized the dollar standard system even more than the GFC of 2007–09 if it had been allowed to develop. Taking these limping aspects of the dollar standard into account, an in-depth analysis of the fundamentals, nature, and present structure of the contemporary dollar standard system since the 2000s must be conducted.

In doing so, we raise three critical questions, which are largely unanswered by the money view: First, what enabled the US dollar to revive its dominance in the 2000s, despite the currency competition with the euro? Second, what drove the US dollar standard system to build up global financial fragility in the 2000s that climaxed with the GFC of 2007–09 being called 'the most severe financial crisis in a century'? And last, what caused the unprecedented sell-off in US Treasury markets, precipitating extraordinary strain on global dollar funding, though a global financial crisis was averted?

Contrary to the main arguments of the money view, this book makes new arguments that the US dollar standard system has developed around shadow banking in the 2000s that proved ultimately destructive in the face of the GFC of 2007–09. It then explores how the dollar standard system underwent a kind of watershed at the height of the COVID-19 financial meltdown. To this end, we focus on the endogenous finance of the global dollar in the shadow banking system backed by US debt securities, particularly US Treasury securities, as collateral assets; this contributes to the dynamic process of the US dollar (USD)-denominated gross balance sheets (liabilities and assets) at global systemically important banks (G-SIBs), based on Hyman H. Minsky and Charles P. Kindleberger's framework on endogenous finance of money.

Part I offers our approach to analyzing the contemporary dollar standard system since the 2000s. Chapter 1 (Introduction) draws attention to the patterns of gross capital flows (inflows and outflows) since the 2000s, which reflect largely USD-denominated gross balance sheets at G-SIBs. Chapter 2 summarizes the characteristics of Minsky and Kindleberger's endogenous finance of money in order to support the arguments that follow.

Part II discusses the fundamentals of the dollar standard system in the 2000s, by analyzing how the dollar could fight off currency competition with the euro in the 2000s. Chapter 3 analyzes how, in the 2000s prior to the GFC of 2007–09, the comparative advantage of the US shadow banking system over the one in the Eurozone encouraged G-SIBs to denominate their gross balance sheets in the dollar rather than the euro.

Part III describes the nature of the dollar standard system in the 2000s, by looking at how endogenous finance of the global dollar in the shadow banking system became more elastic than the traditional banking system in the 2000s prior to the GFC. Chapter 4 argues that the endogenously elastic finance of the global dollar in the shadow banking system facilitated G-SIBs to expand their USD-denominated gross balance sheets in the 2000s. Building on the discussion in Chapter 4, Chapter 5 places particular emphasis on how the endogenously highly elastic financing of the global dollar in the shadow banking system during the US housing bubble (2004–06) drove G-SIBs to overstretch their USD-denominated gross balance sheets that culminated in the GFC of 2007–09.

Based on our approach focusing on the dynamic process of USD-denominated gross balance sheets at G-SIBs, Part IV explores the present structure of the dollar standard system in the 2010s. Chapter 6 discusses how the US Treasury securities serve as universal collateral assets for the endogenous finance of the global dollar in the shadow banking system, which helped G-SIBs expand their USD-denominated gross balance sheets in the 2010s. Chapter 7 discusses how the dollar standard system marks a kind of watershed in the face of the COVID-19 financial turmoil in March 2020. Chapter 8 draws our conclusions.

List of abbreviations

ABCPs	Asset-backed commercial papers
ABSs	Asset-backed securities
ALM	Asset and liability management
AT	Automated trading
BW	Bretton Woods
CCP	Central counterparty
CDOs	Collateralized debt obligations
CLOs	Collateralized loan obligations
COFER	Currency Composition of Official Foreign Exchange Reserves
ECB	European Central Bank
ELA	Emergency liquidity assistance
EMU	Economic and Monetary Union
ETFs	Exchange-traded funds
EU	European Union
EUR	Euro
FICC	Fixed Income Clearing Corporation
FIMA	Foreign and international monetary authorities
FX	Foreign exchange
GC	General collateral
GCF	General collateral finance
GDP	Gross Domestic Product

GFC	Global Financial Crisis
GSEs	Government-sponsored entities
G-SIBs	Global systemically important banks
HFT	High-frequency trading
HQLAs	High-Quality Liquid Assets
IMF	International Monetary Fund
IPE	International Political Economy
LLR	Lender of last resort
MBSs	Mortgage-backed securities
MMMFs	Money market mutual funds
NBFIs	Nonbank financial institutions
NCBs	National central banks
OFCs	Offshore financial centers
OFR	Office of Financial Research
OTD	Originate-to-distribute
PSPP	Public sector purchase program
PTFs	Principal trade firms
QE	Quantitative easing
Repos	Repurchase agreements
SEC	Securities and Exchange Commission
SIFMA	Securities Industry and Financial Markets Association
SIVs	Structured investment vehicles
SPVs	Special purpose vehicles
SWIFT	Society for Worldwide Interbank Financial Telecommunication
TBTF	Too-big-to-fail
USD	US dollar
US Fed	US Federal Reserve

Acknowledgments

I wish to express my deep gratitude to many colleagues, friends, and institutions who have encouraged me to write this book.

Gerald Epstein, Professor of Economics at the University of Massachusetts Amherst (UMass Amherst) and Co-Director of the Political Economy Research Institute (PERI), inspired me to develop the idea of this book. I learned so much from his excellent books and articles on international finance, especially US dollar dominance. He read an earlier draft of this book and since then has given me many valuable comments and suggestions. Without his encouragement and friendship, I never would have been able to write this book. In addition, he and his wife, Francine Deutsch, Prof. Emeritus of Psychology and Education at Mount Holyoke College, MA, have led me to realize how wonderful equally shared parenting with my wife is in my life. Thank you.

Takuyoshi Takada, Emeritus Professor at Chuo University, Tokyo, has taught me a lot about financialization and the Global Financial Crisis (GFC) of 2007–09. His regular briefings about the GFC fueled my writing. He has also given me valuable comments and suggestions to the manuscript. I could not have written this book without his support and patience.

Hasan Cömert, Associate Professor of Economics at Trinity College, CT, encouraged me to write this book. His excellent work on the endogenous process of balance sheet expansion at financial institutions during the US housing bubble (2004–06) convinced me that I should write a book focusing on the dynamics of balance sheet expansion at global banks, which provides us with new arguments for the fundamentals, nature, and present structure of the dollar dominance.

Of course, none of these people are responsible for any of the views I present in this book.

I am extremely grateful to many friends and scholars who have helped me study in the US. The Economics Department and PERI at UMass Amherst invited me as a visiting scholar in 2011 and 2019. Nicole Dunham, PERI's Administrative Director, and Wesley Dunham, Strategic Communication and Program Manager, UMass iCons, have been great friends in the US since

I visited there in the spring of 2011. I also thank their precious children, Eleanor and Adeline. In addition, I thank James Crotty (posthumously) and Michael Ash who welcomed me to the Pioneer Valley. I thank Jong-Seok Oh, Heyon-Kyeong Kim, and Yeohyub Yoon who supported me during my stay at UMass Amherst. Finally, I thank Judy Fogg, PERI's previous Administrative Director, for repeatedly editing my English manuscript. Her excellent work contributed to me revising the manuscript significantly. I could not have written this book without all their support and friendship.

I am indebted to my friends, colleagues, and relatives who helped me and my family living in New York City (NYC) while I finished writing this book. I thank Elizabeth Hay and Stephen Slatin who always treated us as family and whose friendship was critical in helping us relax and be comfortable living in NYC. Thanks to the Economics Department of John Jay College, City University of New York (CUNY), that invited me as a visiting scholar in 2025. In addition, I thank Eunhye Yang, William Bang, and Haeryn Bang, my relatives, who helped us while living in NYC.

I would like to thank scholars and institutions in Japan who contributed to me writing this book. I thank Shoshiro Ogura for coordinating a workshop for financialization whose participants gave me valuable comments and suggestions on an earlier draft. The Economics Department and library at Dokkyo University have supported me for many years, including over the period I have been working on this book.

I thank my brilliant editor at Routledge, Kendrick Loo, and his editorial assistant, Shraddha Saikia, for their support and excellent work in shepherding this book through the publication process. I never could have finished writing it without their patience and understanding. And, I thank two anonymous reviewers for helpful comments and suggestions. Of course, all remaining errors are my responsibility.

Finally, I cannot express sufficiently my enduring gratitude to my wife, Ami Tokunaga, and my son, Jun Tokunaga, who have enthusiastically encouraged me to write this book. I have been greatly inspired by Ami's excellent books on international business such as *Master of Business Administration (MBA)* and *Japanese Business Management* (Gakubunsha, Tokyo). And, I have learned a lot from Jun's enthusiastic discussion on the state of today's US society and the rest of the world, which helped me see this world through younger eyes.

Thank you all.

Part I

Our approach

1 Introduction

1 Literature review on the US dollar standard system

We have been living in the world of the US dollar-centric international monetary system since World War II (WWII). The Bretton Woods (BW) system signed in July 1944 envisioned a gold-dollar standard system that would stabilize the dollar-centric international monetary system after WWII. One of the main features of the gold-dollar standard was a two-tier fixed exchange rate system based on the gold-dollar parity at $35 per ounce. On the one hand, foreign central banks had pegged their currencies to the dollar within plus or minus 1 percent by selling or buying dollar reserves. On the other hand, US monetary authorities had promised to maintain the gold parity at $35 per ounce by selling or buying gold in exchange for their dollar reserves. As such, the gold parity at $35 per ounce functioned as a linchpin for the fixed exchange rate system in the BW system era (Coombs [1976], p.5).

However, on August 15, 1971, US President Richard Nixon unilaterally announced that the US would no longer convert gold stock to foreign central banks for the dollar reserves (i.e., 'Nixon Shock'). In response, foreign central banks, except the US, were not officially required to intervene in foreign exchange markets to peg their own currencies against the dollars, which resulted in the collapse of the fixed exchange rate system in the BW system. Following the Smithsonian Agreement in December 1971, the Committee of Twenty (C-20), created in 1972, tried to forge agreement on a reformed international monetary system. But the C-20 discussion was 'the totally cynical pantomime' for the reform of a stable international monetary system (Strange [1986/2016], p.35). Williamson (1977) attributed the failure of the C-20 negotiations between the US and major developed countries to a lack of political will to cooperate on resolving multinational issues, especially management of the foreign exchange rate. The failure of the C-20 negotiations resulted in a floating exchange rate system, lacking the linchpin of the foreign exchange rate system since 1973. Taking the lack of the linchpin of the exchange rate management into account, Williamson (1976, 1977) proposed the term 'non-system' to characterize the dollar-centric international monetary system

DOI: 10.4324/9781003733959-2

since the breakdown of the BW system. Still, the emergence of the nonsystem was not the end of the US dollar-centric international monetary system, but marked the transition to the 'ad hoc' US dollar standard system because of the lack of alternatives to replace with the dollar (Williamson 1977).

Since the Global Financial Crisis (GFC) of 2007–09, there has been increasing discussion on why the dollar standard system had dominated for 50 years since the collapse of the BW system in the early 1970s.[1] Taken as a whole, the standard discussion proposes seven key criteria determining why the dollar has functioned as a dominant international currency in the post-BW system era: (1) The economic fundamental which is primarily driven by economic size, economic growth, the position in world economy, trade and finance, and international competitiveness; (2) the macroeconomic stability and confidence that results mainly from low inflation and foreign exchange rate stability; (3) large, deep, and liquid financial markets; (4) the political stability and legal fundamental which is largely led by the commitment to open markets, the rule of law, and property rights for foreigners; (5) inertia due to network externalities; (6) supremacy in raw materials market such as petroleum; and (7) great military and geopolitical power.

Building on the discussion, the standard argument has developed taxonomy for characterizing the functions of international currency, which enables us to discern how the US dollar serves as a dominant international money. The standard discussion identifies three functions of money—unit of account, medium of exchange, and store of value—in two sectors: private sector and official sector, for a total of six roles. Based on the classification, the private sector provides separate roles of trade invoicing currency (unit of account), vehicle currency (medium of exchange), and investment and funding currency (store of value). The official level provides anchor currency (unit of account), intervention currency (medium of exchange), and reserve currency (store of value), which was first introduced by Cohen (1971) and Kenen (1983). Although there is not a consolidated and time-series database that provides all the accurate source and information of the six functions of international money, some useful statistics and studies provide an approximate analysis of international usage. Figure 1.1 summarizes currency shares of major currencies in global financial markets.

As illustrated in Figure 1.1, the US dollar accounts for the largest share in all functions of international currency, while the euro ranks second. In particular, some studies have focused on whether the dominance of the dollar as the leading reserve currency is eroded over time. Arslanalp, Eichengreen, and Simpson-Bell (2022) document that the dollar's share of foreign reserves held by central banks and governments has gradually declined since around 2000, based on data from the IMF's Currency Composition of Official Foreign Exchange Reserves (COFER). Despite the ongoing gradual decline, influential academics emphasize that the dollar remains the dominant reserve currency (e.g., Prasad 2014).

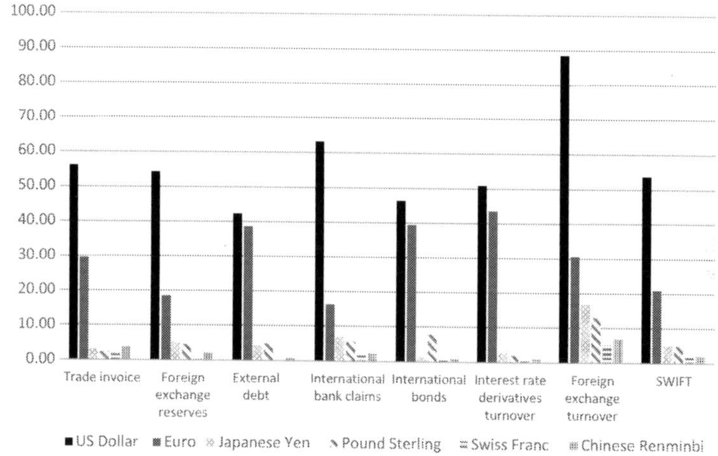

Figure 1.1 The Use of Currencies in International Finance

Sources: Reproduced and revised from McGuire, von Peter and Zhu (2024), Graph 1.B, p.4, p.16.

Notes: Trade invoicing is based on estimated invoicing shares of imports and exports in 2022; foreign exchange (FX) reserves are from IMF's Currency Composition of Official Foreign Exchange Reserves(COFER) are official reserves holdings at the end of 2023; external debt is from Allen, Gautam and Juvenal (2023) external debt liabilities, comprising portfolio debt, foreign direct investment (FDI) debt, and other investment liabilities at the end of 2020; international bank claims are from the BIS locational banking statistics (LBS) by residence at end-2023; international bonds are from the international debt securities (IDS) statistics, amounts outstanding at end-2023; interest rate derivatives turnover is the average daily turnover in OTC interest rate derivatives in April 2022; FX turnover is the average daily turnover in all FX instruments (spot and FX derivatives) in April 2022. Shares add up to 200 percent since FX transactions involve two currencies, and Society for Worldwide Interbank Financial Telecommunication (SWIFT) is the 2023 average of currency shares in international payments excluding intra-eurozone payments.

In order to explain the dominance of the dollar, a growing number of studies by mainstream economists suggests the 'dominant currency paradigm' which analyzes how mutually complementary activities between market participants (banks, nonfinancial corporations, and governments) lead them to use the dominant currency (i.e., the US dollar) for their international trade and transactions. Gopinath and Stein (2018) emphasize the synergies between the use of the dollar in trade and bank-intermediated capital flows, which resulted in strengthening the complementarities between various functions of the dollar as the dominant international money. Based on the analysis, they state that the dollar maintained and, if anything, reinforced its dominance, despite the structural decline in weight of the US in global economy and trade since the 1970s. As such, Pierre-Olivier Gourinchas, a prominent mainstream academic working as an IMF economist, says definitely, "the simple reality is that we live in a dollar world" (Gourinchas [2019], p.2).

In accordance with mainstream academics, International Political Economy (IPE)'s scholars have discussed the international monetary system as a hierarchical structure where the dollar is at the top. Traditionally, IPE's scholars acknowledge the casual primacy of political and geopolitical determinants, i.e., above criteria 6 and 7, without denying the existence of economic determinants of international currency status noted in criteria 1–5.[2] They explain that the US strong military power and dense political and diplomatic alliances, as well as economic determinants, contribute to the maintenance of the dollar-topped international monetary system.[3] Taking data of the dollar's central role in all functions of international money into account (Figure 1.1), there is little or no evidence that any multipolar monetary system consisting of the dollar, the euro, and the Chinese renminbi emerges yet. Based on the findings, the greenback remains as supreme as ever in the international monetary system in the 2010s (Benny and Cohen 2022).

Overall, the standard discussion on international money, including most mainstream economists and IPE scholars, takes the dollar standard system for granted, as the dollar accounts for the largest share in all functions of international currency.

2 The money view in offshore context

Likewise, most heterodox scholars also take the dollar standard system for granted in the post-BW system era. Still, in contrast to the standard discussion emphasizing the dollar's dominance in all functions of international currency, heterodox economists, especially Marxian scholars, have traditionally highlighted that the dollar standard system has an inherently imperial nature. In retrospect, Hudson (1971/2003) proposed a systemic view of the US dollar standard called 'the US Treasury bill standard', which depended on an imperial form of global exploitation. In this form, since the demise of the BW system, foreign central banks in Western Europe and Japan accumulated US Treasury securities, not the form of gold. The replacement of gold by US Treasuries allowed the US to 'automatically' borrow global dollar funds from foreign central banks without reciprocation. Despite the declining position of the US in world economy and trade since the 1970s, the imperial nature of the dollar standard system has been reinforced rather than weakened by its financialization (Panitch and Gindin 2004).[4]

However, the heterodox argument, as well as the standard discussions, has a theoretical blind spot in their analysis, especially by bracketing the importance of the shadow banking system, which has become the center of modern international financial markets. By contrast, the money view, which has become increasingly common in heterodox economists in recent years, provides an alternatively systematic analysis of the dollar standard system by incorporating shadow banking activities into the dollar-topped international monetary system. The money view explains that the entanglement between public and private liabilities/institutions makes the monetary system inherently hierarchical.[5] Different forms of liabilities and institutions are constituted hierarchically within a currency pyramid. Central banks are the top layer of the hierarchy because their liabilities (i.e., central bank reserves) serve as settlement money for commercial banks. The second layer consists of the liabilities of commercial banks (i.e., bank deposits), which serve as settlement money for households and nonfinancial corporations. And the lowest layer consists of the liabilities of nonbank financial institutions (NBFIs), which are often called 'shadow money'.

Some proponents of the money view extend the hierarchical money approach to a global and offshore context. The international domain of issuing dollar liabilities (i.e., global dollar supply) comprises two segments: global dollar supply between residents of US and nonresidents, and offshore dollar supply outside the US. The money view highlights offshore dollar creation outside the US as the key component of the US dollar standard system. In retrospect, global dollar creation outside the US has attracted attention from many scholars and journalists since the 1960s when the Eurodollar market in London has begun to develop rapidly.[6] Eurodollar is, by definition, dollar deposits in a bank or bank branch outside the US, which are, more or less, not subject to US financial regulation. In addition to Eurodollar created by banks, USD-denominated shadow money issued by NBFIs in the offshore realm has increasingly gained importance in global capital flows since the 1970s. The money view regards USD-denominated shadow money in the offshore sphere, combined with Eurodollar, as 'offshore dollar' or 'offshore Eurodollar'.

The discussion of the money view in the offshore context has three distinguishing features.[7] First, the US dollar standard system can be 'taken for granted', in the sense that the contemporary international monetary system is inherently characterized as an international currency hierarchy where the dollar as key currency is at the top and then all other major currencies are pushed down to peripheral positions. Second, the evolution in the hierarchical structure of global dollar liabilities contributes to the US dollar standard's 'systemic nature', despite no defined and agreed official frameworks for stabilizing the dollar-centric international monetary system in the post-BW system era. An important factor sustaining the systemic nature is that the institutional developments in both US financial markets and offshore dollar markets enable USD-denominated offshore and shadow money as the lowest money to be traded at par on demand with the higher US onshore money such as commercial banks' deposits within USD-denominated currency hierarchy. And last, the evolution in the US Federal Reserve (Fed)'s role as international lender of last resort (LLR) since the GFC of 2007–09 allows it to supply the world highest money in the international currency hierarchy (i.e., USD-denominated central bank deposits) without limits to non-US central banks facing dollar shortages. Since the GFC, the Fed expanded the emergency US dollar liquidity provision to non-US central banks with the global swap network initiative.

Furthermore, since the COVID-19 financial turmoil in March 2020, while the Fed extended the swap networks lines with major central banks more broadly, it updated the mechanism of the emergent supply of global dollar liquidity through Foreign and International Monetary Authorities (FIMA) repo facility and Special Drawing Rights (SDRs) system. Such an evolution of the global dollar supply contributes to the 'status quo' dollar standard system where the dollar was dominant in the 2010s.

However, what has emerged in the US dollar standard could not be regarded as an 'invincible' system. First, it is incorrect that the dollar's staying power has always been unrivaled.[8] The US dollar's dominance has, gradually but distinctly, been undermined by the internationalization of the German Deutsche mark and Japanese yen since the second half of the 1980s. In particular, the Deutsch mark as regional key currency replaced the dollar in Europe between the late 1980s and the early 1990s,[9] resulting in the emergence of 'a de-facto Deutschmark zone' that was relatively independent from the US dollar standard system in the early 1990s.[10] With the creation of the euro in 1999, the dominance of the dollar in international debt-financing markets rapidly declined in the 2000s before the GFC. According to the amounts outstanding of international bonds and notes by currency of issue, the percentage accounted for by the US dollar fell from 46.8 percent in December 2000 to 28.8 percent in June 2008, while the euro rose from 29.6 percent to 51.1 percent during the same period. The decline of the role of the dollar is even more dramatic when one looks at the amounts outstanding of the currency composition of international money market instruments. The dollar fell from 87.6 percent in September 1989 to 26.3 percent in June 2008, while the euro rose from 4.4 percent to 48.0 percent during the same period.[11] The rising role of the euro was the first time since the collapse of the BW system that the US dollar standard system faced real currency competition in the 2000s.

Second, the dollar standard system has essentially entailed global financial instability. Looking historically at the US dollar standard system since the 1970s, we can see that the unfettered global capital flows have triggered the recurrence of international currency and monetary crises around the globe that climaxed with the GFC of 2007–09, which had its very epicenter in the US. There were mainly four waves of financial crises: the first wave was in the early 1980s when the Latin American countries defaulted; the second wave was the bursting of the real estate bubble which engulfed Japan in the early 1990s; the third wave was currency and financial crisis in the East Asian countries in 1997–98; and the fourth was the GFC of 2007–09, called 'the most severe financial crisis in a century' (Kindleberger and Aliber 1978/2011).[12]

Finally, the unimaginable dysfunctionality in US Treasury markets at the height of the COVID-19 financial meltdown in March 2020 would have destabilized the dollar standard system even more than the GFC, if it had been allowed to develop. The extraordinary sell-off in US Treasury markets as the largest, deepest, most liquidity financial markets in the world in the face of the COVID-19 financial distress led to an unprecedented pressure of global dollar funding, though a GFC was averted. Taking these limping aspects of the dollar standard system into account, an in-depth analysis of the fundamentals, nature, and present structure of the contemporary dollar standard system since the 2000s must be conducted.[13]

In doing so, we raise three critical questions which are largely unanswered by the money view: What enabled the dollar to revive its dominance in the 2000s, despite the currency competition with the euro? What drove the dollar standard system to contribute to the buildup of global financial fragility in the 2000s that led to the GFC? And finally, what caused the extraordinary selling in US Treasury markets, leading to the unprecedented global dollar funding pressures that would have destabilized the dollar standard system in the face of the COVID-19 financial distress in March 2020?

3 Global capital flows since the 2000s

To respond to these critical questions, it is indispensable to refer to global capital patterns that have been at the center of debates about global financial crises and panics, which many economists and policymakers have drawn attention to since the GFC of 2007–09. In the few years followed by the GFC, a prominent hypothesis is the 'global saving glut' view, which attributes the large imbalances in world current-account positions to the GFC. Since the end of the 1990s, while emerging market countries, predominantly in emerging Asian and oil-exporting countries, have run current-account surpluses, some advanced countries such as the US had expanded current-account deficits. A growing imbalance in world current-account positions emerged in which emerging market countries were consistent providers of net capital flows, and the US was consistently a primary net recipient. Figure 1.2 shows the absolute value of net capital flows, which mirrors the imbalances in the world current account, and gross capital flows (inflow plus outflow between countries) as a percentage of world GDP since 1994.

A sustained increase in net flows started in the second half of the 1990s and peaked at around 5.5 percent in 2006 before the start of the financial crisis. In net capital flows between emerging market countries and the US, large current-account surpluses by emerging market countries, which reflected their domestic excess saving, were channeled into US safe assets such as US Treasury securities, depressing long-term interest rates and fueling the US housing boom there (Bernanke 2005). Crucially, according to the global saving glut view, the GFC was largely triggered by an external and exogenous driver, in the sense that the inflow of excess saving in emerging market countries toward the US contributed to the boom-and-bust cycle there (Bertaut et al. (2011), p.11). Accordingly, this global saving glut view conjectures that the

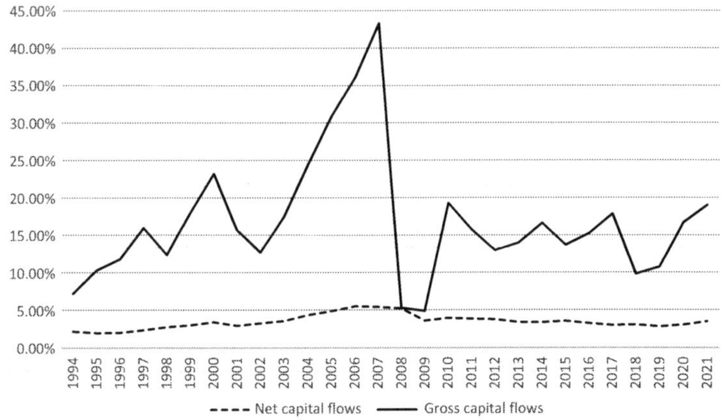

Figure 1.2 Net and Gross Capital Flows (Ratio of World GDP)

Sources: Own elaboration on Battellino (2006), pp.1–2 and Blanchard and Milesi-Ferretti (2009), pp.24 and 27–28, utilizing the IMF Balance of Payments Statistics (BOPS) database and the World Economic Outlook (WEO) database. I thank the staffs at IMF and RBA (Reserve Bank of Australia) who gave useful comments for producing this figure.

Note: In order to highlight the nature of gross capital flows, we sum both gross inflows and outflows, rather than only examining inflows or outflows.

main macroeconomic cause of the GFC is an external and exogenous driver that resulted from excess savings in emerging market countries, not the US shadow banking system that was the epicenter of the GFC.

In the 2010s onward, some economists and policymakers have increasingly suggested that net capital flows, which mirror these global imbalances, are much less important than gross capital flows for understanding the buildup of global financial fragility in the 2000s that led to the GFC.[14] Figure 1.2 demonstrates the absolute value of gross capital flows, which is divided into three periods since the 2000s. First, gross capital flows skyrocketed from 12.7 percent in 2002 to 43.3 percent in 2007 prior to the GFC of 2007–09 and plummeted during the GFC (4.9 percent in 2009).[15] Second, gross capital flows partially rebounded from the bottom of the GFC. Specifically, the volume of gross capital flows bottomed out from 4.9 percent in 2009 to 19.3 percent in 2010. Lastly, gross capital flows recovered but remained below their pre-GFC trend in the 2010s (hovering around 10 percent and 15 percent for the most part), though it fluctuated from year to year.

With the largest role of the US dollar in international trade and finance mentioned above (Figure 1.1), most gross capital flows are denominated in the dollar. The majority of gross capital flows denominated in the dollar are conducted by a handful of global systemically important banks (G-SIBs) or large complex financial institutions (LCFIs), also known as 'megabanks' or 'big banks' (Parchimowicz 2023). G-SIBs in the US and Europe dominate global financial markets for banking, debt and equity securities, syndicated loans, securitizations, structured-finance products, and OTC derivatives in the world (Caparusso et al. 2019).[16]

Given the dominant position of G-SIBs in international financial markets, the movement of the USD-denominated gross capital flows largely reflected the growth of USD-denominated gross balance sheets (liabilities plus assets) on a global scale at G-SIBs. In particular, large European banks expanded their gross balance sheets denominated in the dollar significantly in the 2000s prior to GFC. As Figure 1.3 shows, outstanding USD-denominated assets and liabilities at European banks had significantly increased since about 2000, and both reached above $12 trillion in 2008.

Focusing on the dynamic growth of USD-denominated gross balance sheets at G-SIBs provides us with new arguments for the fundamentals, nature, and present structure of the US dollar standard system since the 2000s, which are largely unexplored by the money view. To this end, we shed light

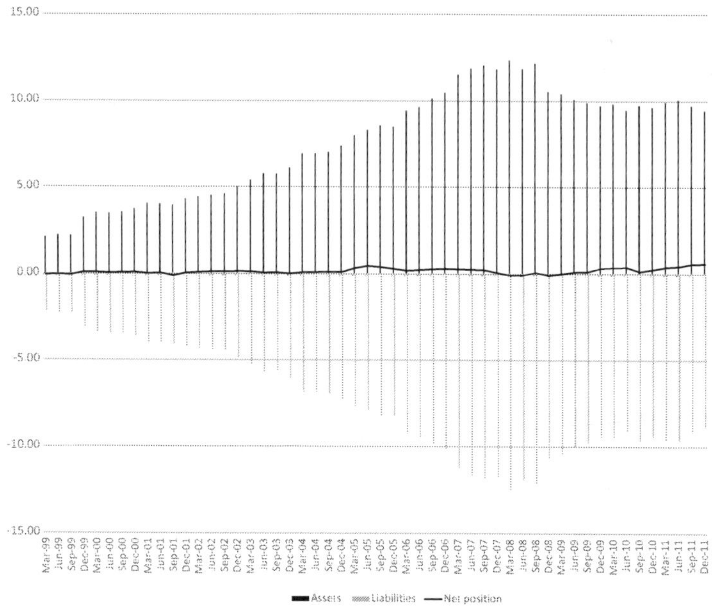

Figure 1.3 Net Position and Gross Balance Sheets Denominated in the US Dollar of European Banks ($ Trillion: Quarterly)

Sources: Own elaboration on data from McGuire, von Peter and Zhu (2024), Graph 8.A, p.13; BIS consolidated banking statistics.

Notes: Bank's intragroup positions are included. European banks consist of Eurozone countries, the United Kingdom, and Switzerland.

on the endogenous finance of the global dollar in the unregulated and shadow banking system backed by US debt securities, especially US Treasury securities, as collateral assets, which contribute to the dynamic process of USD-denominated gross balance sheets at G-SIBs. In doing so, we discuss the characteristics of Minsky and Kindleberger's framework on endogenous finance of money in a closed economy in Chapter 2.

Notes

1 There is a huge literature on argument of why the US dollar has been used as a leading international currency over many decades. See Bergstein (1975); Kenen (1983); Yamamoto (1988, 1994); Tavlas (1992); Hartmann (1998); Portes (2010); Eichengreen (2011); Cohen (2015); Gourinchas, Rey, and Sauzet (2019); Gourinchas (2019); Epstein (2019, Chapter 3); CGFS (2020); Bertaut, von Beschwitz and Curcuru (2023); Fried (2023).

2 For example, Strange (1971); Cohen (1998).

3 Though few IPE studies suggest the expectations that international monetary system is in motion from the unipolar dollar standard system into a multipolar system with the dollar, the euro, and the Chinese renminbi since the 2010s (Eichengreen 2011; Eichengreen, Mehl and Chitu 2018), most of IPE's academics takes the dollar standard system for granted. With respect to the latter, special issue, 'Focus on the International Currency System', Review of International Political Economy (RIPE), vol. no.5, October 2014 is a representative collection of IPE's articles debating the dollar-topped currency hierarchy approach in the post-BW system era.

4 In addition, it has been debated among many heterodox scholars why the dollar's hegemony remains since the collapse of the BW system, particularly the GFC of 2007–09. The discussion includes neo-Cartelist approach (e.g., Field and Vernengo 2013), post-Keynesian currency hierarchy approach (e.g., Prates 2020), post-Keynesian structural approach (e.g., Palley 2022), and the hypothesis of financial securities as commodities (e.g., Kaltenbrunner and Lysandrou 2017). Since the 2020s, there has been increasing discussion among heterodox economists on 'the de-dollarization', highlighting the decline in the dollar's dominance in foreign exchange reserves, which implies that the contemporary international monetary system is transitioning away from the unipolar dollar standard system toward the multipolar currency world (e.g., Bush et al. 2023). But most of them also largely bracket the rise of shadow banking system in their analysis, which we argue in the book.

5 Mehrling (2010, 2011, 2012, 2015, 2016); Mehrling et al. (2013); Pozsar (2014, 2015); Murau (2017).

6 Einzig (1964); Bell (1973); Dufey and Giddiy (1978); Helleiner (1994); Burn (2006); Shaxson (2011, 2019); Norfiled (2016).

7 Mehrling (2015, 2016); Murau (2018, 2020); Murau, Rini and Haas (2018, 2020); Murau and Pforr (2020); Murau, Pape and Pforr (2021, 2022).

8 Epstein (2019), p.54.

9 Inoue (1994); Yamamoto (1994).

10 De Grauwe (1991).

11 Own estimations from BIS Debt Securities Statistics database.

12 In contrast to the advocates of the money view in the Western world, many heterodox scholars in emerging and developing countries have criticized that the uncontrolled and speculative flows of offshore Eurodollar have contributed to the nonsystemic and destabilizing nature of the US dollar standard system (e.g., Sundaram 2011; Ocampo 2017).

13 Aliber (1973) and McKinnon (1974) suggested the term 'limping dollar standard'.

14 Borio and Disyatat (2011); Dorrucci and McKay (2011); Milesi-Ferretti and Tille (2011); Obstfeld (2012); Shin (2012); Tokunaga and Epstein (2014, 2018); Bonizzi (2016).

15 Gross debt-financing flows have largely driven the volume of gross capital flows in the 2000s before the GFC. Gross debt-financing flows, including portfolio and other (i.e., banking) investment flows, were extremely volatile in comparison to foreign direct investment (FDI) and equity investment.

16 The Financial Stability Board (FSB) has annually updated the list of G-SIBs since 2011. The list of 2023 includes 29 G-SIBs in the US, Europe, Japan, Canada, China, and Hong Kong.

References

Aliber, R.Z. (1973), "National Preferences and the Scope for International Monetary Reform", *Essays in International Finance*, Princeton University, no.101, November 1973.

Allen, C., D. Gautam, and L. Juvenal (2023), "Currencies of External Balance Sheets", *IMF Working Papers*, International Monetary Fund (IMF), 23/237, November 2023.

Arslanalp, S., B. Eichengreen, and C. Simpson-Bell (2022), "The Stealth Erosion of Dollar Dominance: Active Diversifiers and the Rise of Nontraditional Reserve Currencies", *IMF Working Paper*, International Monetary Fund (IMF), 22/058, March 2022.

Battellino, R. (2006), "Regional Capital Flows", *Reserve Bank Bulletin*, Reserve Bank of Australia (RBA), July 2006.

Bell, G. (1973), *The Euro-Dollar Market and the International Financial System*, New York: Wiley.

Benny, T.M. and B.J. Cohen (2022), "The International Currency System Revisited", *Review of Keynesian Economics*, vol.10, issue 4, pp.443–461.

Bergstein, C.F. (1975), *The Dilemmas of the Dollar: The Economics and Politics of United States International Monetary Policy*, New York: New York University Press.

Bernanke, B.S. (2005), The Global Saving Glut and the US Current Account Deficit, Speech at the Sandridge Lecture, Virginia Association of Economics, Richmond, VA, Board of Governors of the Federal Reserve System, March 10, 2005.

Bertaut, C., L.P. DeMarco, S. Kamin, and R. Tryon (2011), "ABS Inflows to the United States and the Global Financial Crisis", *International Finance Discussion Papers*, Board of Governors of the Federal Reserve System, no.1028, August 2011.

Bertaut, C., B. von Beschwitz, and S. Curcuru (2023), ""The International Role of the US Dollar" Post-COVID Edition", *FEDS Notes*, Board of Governors of the Federal Reserve System, June 23, 2023.

Blanchard, O. and G.M. Milesi-Ferretti (2009), "Global Imbalances: In Midstream?" *Staff Position Note*, International Monetary Fund (IMF), SPN09/29, October 2009.

Bonizzi, B. (2016), Institutional Investors and Capital Flows to Emerging Markets, School of Oriental and African Studies (SOAS), University of London.

Borio, C. and P. Disyatat (2011), "Global Imbalances and the Financial Crisis: Link or No Link?" *BIS Working Papers*, Bank for International Settlements (BIS), no.346, May 2011.

Burn, G. (2006), *The Re-Emergence of Global Finance*, Basingstoke: Palgrave Macmillan.

Bush, S.B., N. Bukhari, J. Cordova, N. Ingram, K. Kabela, J. Kai, and V. Tapia (2023), "Will the World Ditch the Dollar?", *Dollar & Sense*, September/October 2023, pp.11–21.

Caparusso, J., C.Y. Chen, P. Dattels, R. Goel, and P. Hiebert (2019), "Post-Crisis Changes in Global Bank Business Models: A New Taxonomy", *IMF Working Paper*, International Monetary Fund (IMF), 19/295, December 2019.

Cohen, B.J. (1971), *The Future of Sterling as an International Currency*, London: Macmillan.

Cohen, B.J. (1998), *The Geography of Money*, Ithaca, NY: Cornell University Press.

Cohen, B.J. (2015), *Currency Power: Understanding Monetary Rivalry*, Princeton, NJ: Princeton University Press.

Committee on the Global Financial System (CGFS) (2020), "US Dollar Funding: An International Perspective", *CGFS Papers*, Bank for International Settlements (BIS), no.65, June 2020.

Coombs, C.A. (1976), *The Arena of International Finance*, New York: Wiley.

De Grauwe, P. (1991), "Is the European Monetary System a DM-Zone?" in Steinherr, A. and, D. Weiserbs (eds.), Evolution of the International and Regional Monetary Systems: Essays in Honour of Robert Triffin, London: Palgrave Macmillan, pp.207–227.

Dorrucci, E. and J. McKay (2011), "The International Monetary System after the Financial Crisis", *Occasional Paper Series*, European Central Bank (ECB), no.123, February 2011.

Dufey, G. and I.H. Giddiy (1978), *The International Money Market*, Englewood Cliffs, NJ: Prentice-Hall.

Eichengreen, B. (2011), *Exorbitant Privilege: The Rise and Fall of the Dollar and the Future of the International Monetary System*, New York: Oxford University Press.

Eichengreen, B., A. Mehl, and L. Chitu (2018), *How Global Currencies Work: Past, Present, and Future*, Princeton, NJ: Princeton University Press.

Einzig, P. (1964), *The Euro-Dollar System: Practice and Theory of International Interest Rates*, London: Macmillan.

Epstein, G. (2019), *What's Wrong with Modern Monetary Theory? A Policy Critique*, Cham: Palgrave Macmillan.

Fields, D. and M. Vernengo (2013), "Hegemonic Currencies during the Crisis: The Dollar versus the Euro in a Cartalist Perspective", *Review of International Political Economy*, vol.20, issue 4, pp.740–759.

Fried, D. (2023), "The US Dollar as an International Currency and Its Economic Effects", *Working Paper*, Congressional Budget Office (CBO), no.2023–04, April 17, 2023.

Gopinath, G. and J.C. Stein (2018), "Banking, Trade, and the Making of a Dominate Currency", *NBER Working Paper*, National Bureau of Economic Research (NBER), no.24485, April 2018.

Gourinchas, P. (2019), The Dollar Hegemon? Evidence and Implications for Policymakers, Prepared for the 6th Asian Monetary Policy Forum held on May 31, 2019, Singapore.

Gourinchas, P., H. Rey and M. Sauzet (2019), "The International Monetary and Financial System", *NBER Working Paper*, National Bureau of Economic Research (NBER), no.25782, April 2019.

Hartmann, P. (1998), *Currency Competition and Foreign Exchange Markets: The Dollar, the Yen and the Euro*, Cambridge: Cambridge University Press.

Helleiner, E. (1994), *States and the Reemergence of Global Finance: From Bretton Woods to the 1990s*, Ithaca, NY: Cornell University Press.

Hudson, H. (1971/2003), *Super Imperialism: The Origin and Fundamentals of US World Dominance*, Second Edition, London: Pluto Press.

Inoue, I. (1994), *International Currencies in Europe and Asia*, Tokyo: Nihon Keizai Hyoronsha (in Japanese).

Kaltenbrunner, A. and P. Lysandrou (2017), "The US Dollar's Continuing Hegemony as an International Currency: A Double-Matrix Analysis", *Development and Change*, vol.48, issue 4, pp.663–691.

Kenen, P. (1983), "The Role of the Dollar as an International Currency", *Occasional Papers*, Group of Thirty, no.13.

Kindleberger, C.P. and R.Z. Aliber (1978/2011), *Manias, Panics, and Crashes: A History of Financial Crises,* Sixth Edition, New York: Palgrave Macmillan.

McGuire, P., G. von Peter and S. Zhu (2024), "International Finance through the Lens of BIS Statistics: The Global Reach of Currencies", *BIS Quarterly Review*, Bank for International Settlements (BIS), June 10, 2024, pp.1–16.

McKinnon, R.I. (1974), "A New Tripartite Monetary Agreement or a Limping Dollar Standard?" *Essays in International Finance*, Princeton University, no.106, October 1974.

Mehrling, P. (2010), Money and Empire: A Biography of the Dollar, A Proposal for the Institute for New Economic Thinking (INET), July 28, 2010.

Mehrling, P. (2011), *The New Lombard Street: How the Fed Became the Dealer of Last Resort*, Princeton, NJ: Princeton University Press.

Mehrling, P. (2012), "The Inherent Hierarchy of Money", in L. Taylor, A. Rezai, T. Michl (eds.), *Social Fairness and Economics: Economic Essays in the Spirit of Duncan Foley*, New York: Routledge, pp.394–404.

Mehrling, P. (2015), "Elasticity and Discipline in the Global Swap Network", *Working Papers*, Institute for New Economic Thinking (INET), no.27, November 2015.

Mehrling, P. (2016), "Beyond Bancor", *Challenge*, vol.59, issue 1, pp.22–34.

Mehrling, P., Z. Pozsar, J. Sweeney, and D.H. Nielson (2013), Bagehot Was a Shadow Banker: Shadow Banking, Central Banking, and the Future of Global Finance, November 5, 2013.

Milesi-Ferretti, G.M. and C. Tille (2011), "The Great Retrenchment: International Capital Flows during the Global Financial Crisis", *Economic Policy*, vol.26, issue 66, pp.285–342.

Murau, S. (2017), "Shadow Money and the Public Money Supply: The Impact of the 2007–2009 Financial Crisis on the Monetary System", *Review of International Political Economy*, vol.24, issue 5, pp.802–838.

Murau, S. (2018), "Offshore Dollar Creation and the Emergence of the Post-2008 International Monetary System", Institute for Advanced Sustainability Studies (IASS) Discussion Paper, June 2018.

Murau, S. (2020), "A Macro-Financial Model of the Eurozone Architecture Embedded in the Global Offshore USD System", *GEGI Study*, Global Economic Governance Initiative (GEGI), Global Development Policy Center, Boston University, July 2020.

Murau, S., J. Rini and A. Haas (2018), "The Future of Offshore Dollar Creation: Four Scenarios for the International Monetary System by 2040", *Institute for Advanced Sustainability Studies (IASS) Discussion Paper*, June 2018.

Murau, S., J. Rini and A. Haas (2020), "The Evolution of the Offshore US-Dollar System: Past, Present and Four Possible Futures", *Journal of Institutional Economics*, vol.16, issue 6, pp.767–783.

Murau, S. and T. Pforr (2020), "What is Money in a Critical Macro-Finance Framework? *Finance and Society*, vol.6, issue 1, pp.56–66.

Murau, S., F. Pape and T. Pforr (2021), "The Hierarchy of the Offshore US-Dollar System: On Swap Lines, the FIMA Repo Facility and Special Rights", *GEGI Study*, Global Economic Governance Initiative (GEGI), Global Development Policy Center, Boston University, February 2021.

Murau, S., F. Pape and T. Pforr (2022), "International Monetary Hierarchy through Emergency US-dollar Liquidity: A Key Currency Approach", *Competition & Change*, vol.27, issue 3–4, pp.495–515.

Norfiled, T. (2016), *The City: London and the Global Power of Finance*, London: Verso.

Obstfeld, M. (2012), "Does the Current Account Still Matter?" *American Economic Review*, Papers and Proceedings, vol.102, issue 3, pp.1–23.

Ocampo, J.A. (2017), *Resetting the International Monetary (Non) System*, Oxford: Oxford University Press.

Palley, T. (2022), "Theorizing Dollar Hegemony: The Political Economic Foundations of Exorbitant Privilege", *Review of Keynesian Economics*, vol.10, no.4, pp.462–498.

Panitch, L. and S. Gindin (2004), "Finance and American Empire", in L. Panitch and C. Leys (eds.), The Empire Reloaded: Socialist Register, London: Merlin Press, vol.41, pp.46–81.

Parchimowicz, K.M. (2023), *The Regulation of Megabanks: Legal Frameworks of the USA and EU*, Abingdon, Oxon: Routledge.

Portes, R. (2010), Global Crisis and International Currencies, Economic and Social Research Institute, Cabinet Office, Government of Japan, March 2010.

Pozsar, Z. (2014), "Shadow Banking: The Money View", *Working Paper*, Office of Financial Research (OFR), 14-04, July 2, 2014.

Pozsar, Z. (2015), A Macro View of Shadow Banking. Levered Betas and Wholesale Funding in the Context of Secular Stagnation, January 31, 2015, available at SSRN: https://ssrn.com/abstract=2558945 or https://dx. doi.org/10.2139/ssrn.2558945

Prasad, E. (2014), *The Dollar Trap: How the US Dollar Tightened its Grip on Global Finance*, Princeton, NJ: Princeton University Press.

Prates, D. (2020), "Beyond Modern Money Theory: A Post-Keynesian Approach to the Currency Hierarchy, Monetary Sovereignty, and Policy Space", *Review of Keynesian Economics*, vol.8, no.4, pp.494–511.

Shaxson, N. (2011), *Treasure Islands: Tax Havens and the Men Who Stole the World*, New York: St. Martin's Press.

Shaxson, N. (2019), *The Finance Curse: How Global Finance Is Making Us All Poorer*, New York: Grove Press.

Shin, H.S. (2012), "Global Banking Glut and Loan Risk Premium", *IMF Economic Review*, International Monetary Fund (IMF), vol.60, issue 2, pp.155–192.

Strange, S. (1971), *Sterling and British Policy: A Political Study of an International Currency in Decline*, London and New York: Oxford University Press.

Strange, S. (1986/2016), *Casino Capitalism*, Manchester: Manchester University Press.

Sundaram, J.K. (ed.) (2011), *Reforming the International Financial System for Development*, New York: Columbia University Press.

Tavlas, G.S. (1992), "Vehicle Currency", in P. Newman, M. Milgate and J. Eatwell (eds.), *The Palgrave Dictionary of Money & Finance*, no.3, London: Macmillan, pp.754–757.

Tokunaga, J. and G. Epstein (2014), "The Endogenous Finance of Global Dollar-Based Financial Fragility in the 2000s: A Minskian Approach", *PERI Working Paper*, Political Economy Research Institute (PERI), University of Massachusetts Amherst, no.340, January 2014.

Tokunaga, J. and G. Epstein (2018), "The Endogenous Finance of Global-Dollar-Based Financial Fragility in the 2000s: A Minskyan Approach", *Review of Keynesian Economics*, vol.6, no.1, January 2018, pp.62–82.

Williamson, J. (1976), "The Benefits and Costs of an International Monetary System", in E.M. Bernstein et al., Reflections on Jamanica, *Essays in International Finance*, Princeton University, no.115, April 1976, pp.54–59.

Williamson, J. (1977), *The Failure of World Monetary Reform, 1971–74*, New York: New York University Press.

Yamamoto, E. (1988), *The Replacement of Key Currency and the US Dollar*, Tokyo: Yuhikaku (in Japanese).

Yamamoto, E. (1994), *The German Mark and Japanese Yen Under 'the US Dollar Standard System'*, Tokyo: Nihon Keizai Hyoronsha (in Japanese).

2 Minsky and Kindleberger's framework on endogenous finance of money

1 Asset and liability management strategy

Hyman H. Minsky provided a heterodox model called 'financial fragility hypothesis' (Kregel 2013), in which financial institutions, particularly banks, play a critical role in the endogenous transformation of the financial system as a whole from robustness to fragility that can lead to a financial crisis in a closed economy.[1] Some journalists and policymakers who focus on Minsky's framework claimed that the Global Financial Crisis (GFC) of 2007–09 can be characterized as a 'Minsky moment', echoing Minsky's classification of three balance-sheet postures: hedge finance, speculative finance, and Ponzi finance. By contrast, some post-Keynesian economists insist that the financial crisis cannot be recognized as such a moment (these include Davidson [2008] and Kregel [2010]). They argue that the central fundamental idea of Minsky's framework is the endogenous finance of money, contributing to the buildup of financial fragility that leads to financial crises (Nesvetailova 2010), rather than specifically applying Minsky's classification of three balance-sheet postures to analyze financial crises.

Based on Minsky's framework, Charles P. Kindleberger constructed a model that a full-blown mania goes to financial crises through the sequence of five stages: displacement, euphoria, distress, panic, and crash. His model, called often by 'Minsky-Kindleberger model' (Mehrling 2023), started with his classic book: *Manias, Panics, and Crashes* (first edition, published in 1978) which gave a detailed account of perennial financial crises in the world for the last 400 years. In this book, Kindleberger sketched that almost every mania was fueled by the endogenous finance of money and credit rather than exogenous factors and events (Kindleberger and Aliber [1978/2011], p.64). While Minsky and Kindleberger had different views in terms of the mechanism of economy from robustness toward fragile, they shared an intellectual tradition that the endogenous finance of money plays a central role in the dynamic transformation of the financial system to increase financial fragility that leads to financial crisis.[2]

DOI: 10.4324/9781003733959-3

Clearly, the two distinguished economists' framework on endogenous finance of money would have obvious implications for understanding the buildup of global financial fragility that led to the GFC of 2007–09 and the COVID-19 financial distress in March 2020. In this chapter, we summarize the characteristics of Minsky and Kindleberger's framework on endogenous finance of money in a closed economy, which helps us frame the arguments that follow.[3]

Minsky primarily explains how nonfinancial corporations increase credit demand from banks, as the relationship between cash flows and liabilities changes over the business cycle. He proposes three corporate balance-sheet postures, as mentioned above, which lead to the endogenous transformation of the economy from financial robustness to fragility (Minsky [1986b/2008], pp.230–238). Nonfinancial corporations increase credit demands from banks, as the deterioration of their balance sheets transforms them from hedge finance to speculative or Ponzi finance units. In response, banks accommodate credit demand from nonfinancial corporations, resulting in money supply growth in the financial system (Minsky [1982], xx). In short, money supply is endogenously determined, not exogenously controlled by central banks (Minsky [1986b/2008], pp.252–253; Kindleberger and Aliber [1978/2011], p.64).

Notably, banks, the central financial institutions of capitalist economies, not only passively accommodate credit demand from nonfinancial corporations but also, more importantly, actively expand their gross balance sheets for maximizing their profits (Minsky [1986b/2008], pp.256–257; Minsky [1992], p.6). With respect to the latter, banks seek to raise their profits by discovering ways of increasing the return on their assets or decreasing the cost of their liabilities (Minsky [1986b/2008], p.81). In doing so, they develop asset and liability management (ALM) strategies, accelerating their tendencies to develop new financial innovations and instruments (Minsky [1986b/2008], p.354), which change the main compositions on each side of banks' gross balance sheets (liabilities plus assets) characterized by the traditional and commercial banking system.

On the asset side of gross balance sheets, banks search for eligible assets with a relatively high-yield alternative to traditional banking lending. To this end, banks expand securitization activity which enables them to create new eligible asset alternatives to traditional lending and loans. Minsky called securitization a 'hot' financial development to illustrate his concept of the financial fragility hypothesis (Minsky [1986c], p.4). Securitization decouples a single financial intermediation in the traditional and commercial banking system into various steps. In bank financing, financial intermediation between lending and borrowing is conducted by one entity, i.e., the bank. In the securitization activity, by contrast, bank lending or loans could be transformed into longer and more multiple chains of eligible securities and financial instruments that are sold on financial markets (Minsky [1986c], pp.24–25; Minsky

[1988], pp.24–25).[4] Thus, the development of securitization allows banks to create eligible assets with relatively high-yield alternatives to bank lending and loans.

On the liability side of gross balance sheets, banks are motivated to develop new financial innovations and instruments for creating short-term liability alternatives to insured bank deposits (Kindleberger and Aliber [1978/2011], pp.62–65; Minsky [1986b/2008], p.81). The development of new financial innovations and instruments facilitates the emergence of liberalized and unregulated banking activity that is not channeled through the commercial and regulated banking system. Banks promote the creation of a number of different types of private money, including repurchase agreements (repos), certificates of deposit (CDs), and offshore Eurodollar market borrowing, as alternatives to insured bank deposits (Minsky [1986b/2008], pp.82–87). The development of a number of different types of private money drives the endogenous supply of money to become more elastic in the unregulated banking systems than in the regulated banking system; this dynamic leads to an increase in the rate at which the existing supply of money is exchanged in an economy, i.e., the velocity of money (Minsky [1975/2008], p.120; Minsky [1982], pp.141–142). The rise in velocity of money contributes to a permanent increase in banks' lending ability (Minsky [1982], p.172).[5] Hence, banks develop new financial innovations and instruments that drive the endogenous finance of money to become more elastic in the unregulated banking systems than that of the regulated banking system backstopped by central banks.

Overall, the aggressive pursuit of ALM strategy on each side of gross balance sheets at banks leads to the development of financial intermediation through the liberalized and unregulated banking system, which is relatively independent from the traditional banking system that is ultimately regulated by central banks. The new banking system was dubbed 'the second banking' (Minsky [1982], p.141) or 'the parallel banking system' (D'Arista and Schlesinger 1993), but is now more commonly referred to as the 'shadow banking system' (McCulley 2009), which is much less regulated than the traditional banking system.

2 Procyclical mechanism of gross balance sheets during euphoria

Minsky argued that the secular success of financial markets, the persistent absence of serious financial difficulties, and the improvement of expectations would lead to the advent of euphoria, "in which increasing short-term financing of long positions becomes a normal way of life" (Minsky [1986b/2008], p.237). During euphoria, banks increasingly come to rely on collateralized short-term borrowing such as repos in the unregulated and shadow banking system, rather than borrowing based on cash flows in the regulated and traditional banking system. While government bonds serve as collateral assets in repos, nongovernment securities could also function as collateral (Minsky [1982], p.171). Notably, collateralized-based borrowing is essentially more volatile in the unregulated banking system than loans based on the value of the cash flows that are expected from income-earning operations in the regulated banking system, in that the viability of collateralized short-term borrowing depends on the expected market value of the pledged collateral assets (Minsky [1986b/2008], pp.260–261).

In addition, a procyclical mechanism exists in banks' gross balance sheets during euphoria. The endogenous supply of money and credit increases rapidly in boom or euphoria and decreases sharply during downturn (Kindleberger and Aliber [1978/2011], pp.26–27, p.65). With respect to the former, the procyclical mechanism would encourage the endogenous finance of money to become highly elastic during euphoria, allowing banks to pursue excessive leverage and risk-taking for purchasing long-term assets, which contributes to the rapid expansion of their gross balance sheets.

Importantly, the dynamic process in the endogenous supply of money leads the financial system as a whole to become fragile. This is because it entails greater vulnerability to drastic changes in expected market values of collateral assets, supported by euphoric expectations and the underestimation of risk. Minsky stresses that financial fragility, which is a prerequisite for financial instability and financial crisis, is inherent in internal market processes in liberalized and unregulated banking systems (Minsky [1986b/2008], p.280).

Finally, during euphoria associated with mania, asset prices decline suddenly after they stop increasing. Once asset prices tumble sharply, the dash for liquidity may drive the sale of assets in the distressed circumstances, which trigger further declines in their prices (Kindleberger and Aliber [1978/2011], pp.13, 15). The procyclical mechanism during the downturn leads to the collapse in value of collateral assets, precipitating pressure on the endogenous finance of money in the unregulated banking system that would shrink their gross balance sheets drastically. As such, the dynamic and ultimately destructive process of gross balance sheets at the banks results in financial crisis.

3 Characteristics of Minsky and Kindleberger's framework

To summarize the characteristics of Minsky and Kindleberger's framework on the endogenous finance of money in a closed economy, three features are worth noting: (1) the pursuit of ALM strategies at banks, (2) the endogenously elastic finance of money in the unregulated banking system, and (3) the highly elastic endogenous supply of money during euphoria.

First, the aggressive pursuit of the ALM strategies at banks accelerates their tendencies to develop new financial innovations and instruments, which enable them to create new eligible assets and short-term liabilities in the unregulated banking system, contributing to the expansion of banks' gross balance sheets. Second, the expansion of gross balance sheets at banks is driven by their reliance on creating a number of different types of private money such as repos on the liability side—i.e., the endogenously elastic finance of money backed by collateral assets in the unregulated banking system. Third, the highly elastic endogenous supply of money in the shadow banking system, driven by the procyclical mechanism in banks' gross balance sheets during euphoria, accelerates to rapidly expand their gross balance sheets. Crucially, the rising market value of the pledged collateral assets determines how highly elastic the endogenous finance of money in the unregulated banking system becomes during euphoria, overstretching banks' gross balance sheets. By contrast, the collapse of collateral assets during downturns causes pressure on the endogenous finance of money in the unregulated banking system that would decrease their gross balance sheets rapidly, leading to financial crisis.

In the following chapters, we will discuss the three features in the global context, enabling us to understand the endogenously dynamic process of USD-denominated gross balance sheets (liabilities and assets) at global systemically important banks (G-SIBs) since the 2000s.[6] More specifically, based on the first feature (i.e., the pursuit of the ALM strategies at banks), we analyze why G-SIBs denominated gross balance sheets in the dollar, rather than the euro, in the 2000s (Chapter 3). Based upon the second feature (i.e., the endogenously elastic finance of money in the unregulated banking system), we discuss what led G-SIBs to expand their USD-denominated gross balance sheets in the 2000s (Chapter 4). Regarding the third feature (i.e., the highly elastic endogenous supply of money during euphoria), we discuss what drove G-SIBs to overstretch their USD-denominated gross balance sheets during the US housing bubble (2004–06) that climaxed with the GFC of 2007–09 (Chapter 5).

Building on our approach focusing on the endogenously dynamic process of USD-denominated gross balance sheets at G-SIBs, we describe what contributed to G-SIBs recovering their USD-denominated gross balance sheets in the 2010s, which remained below the pre-GFC trend (Chapter 6); further, we discuss what precipitated unprecedented pressure on the global dollar supply at the height of the COVID-19 financial distress in March 2020, which would, *ceteris paribus*, have resulted in the collapse of their USD-denominated gross balance sheets (Chapter 7).

Notes

1 Minsky and many of his post-Keynesian followers have presented in common the financial fragility hypothesis in single and closed economy dimensions (Strange [1986/2016], p.65). Meanwhile, as Wray (2006) proposes, Minsky (1979, 1986a) gave only a short account of the position of the US in global economy and finance as a 'world banker', which Despres, Kindleberger, and Salant (1966) suggested in the 1960s. Moreover, Minsky (1991), as Mehrling (1999) and Nesvetailova (2007) suggest, pointed out that the US has become a Ponzi unit since the second half of

the 1980s, in the sense that it has borrowed in international capital markets to pay the interest as well as the principle on its external debt, which mirrors the massive accumulation of its current-account deficit.

2 But Kindlerberger was careful to distance himself from Minsky's goes-too-far emphasizing the inherent financial fragility (Mehrling [2022], pp.206–207).

3 We here explain the characteristics of Minsky and Kindleberger' framework, based on the studies of a post-Keynesian's theory of structural endogeneity (such as Pollin 1991 and Dymski and Pollin 1992), which focuses on how the endogenous finance of money in unregulated financial markets accelerates the transformation of the financial system from robustness toward fragility and leads to financial crisis.

4 In the longer and more multiple financial intermediation than the simple intermediation in the traditional banking system, dealer banks can be regarded as an essential player to interface with many different types of entities (Minsky [1986c], pp.24–25; Minsky [1987], p.7; Minsky [1988], pp.24–25).

5 This dynamic in the endogenous finance of money can be understood as "a perpetuum mobile; the history of money is a story of continuing innovations so that the existing supply of money can be used more efficiently and the development of close substitutes for money that circumvent the regulatory requirements applied to the creation of money" (Kindleberger and Aliber [1978/2011], p.65).

6 There has been an increasing discussion about extending the Minsky financial fragility hypothesis in a closed economy into the global context. Kindleberger (1978/2005, 1988) and Gray and Gray (1994) were pioneering studies which developed Minsky's perspective for examining global financial instability. Since the East Asian financial crisis in the late 1990s, some post-Keynesian economists have focused on applying Minsky's classification of three balance-sheet postures into the global context in order to explain the endogenous transformation of the financial system in these regions toward fragility, leading to the financial crisis there (Kregel 1998; Dymski 1999; Arestis and Glickman 2002; Schroeder 2002; Wolfson 2002; Nesvetailova 2007). By contrast, Frenkel and Rapetti (2009) argue that the elements that have accelerated the boom in the developing countries since the late 1970s are exogenous in nature, while the factors that triggered the boom in the subprime financial crisis in the US can be essentially understood as endogenous.

References

Arestis, P. and M. Glickman (2002), "Financial Crisis in Southeast Asia: Dispelling Illusion the Minskyan Way", *Cambridge Journal of Economics*, vol.26, issue 2, pp.237–260.

D'Arista, J.W. and T. Schlesinger (1993), "The Parallel Banking System", in G. Dymski, G. Epstein, and R. Pollin (eds.), *Transforming the US Financial System: Equity and Efficiency for the 21st Century*, Armonk, NY: ME Sharpe, pp.157–199.

Davidson, P. (2008), "Is the Current Financial Distress Caused by the Subprime Mortgage Crisis a Minsky Moment? Or Is It the Result of Attempting to Securitize Illiquid Noncommercial Mortgage Loans?" *Journal of Post Keynesian Economics*, vol.30, issue 4, pp.669–676.

Despres, E., C.P. Kindleberger and W. Salant (1966), "The Dollar and World Liquidity: A Minority View", *The Economist*, February 5, 1966.

Dymski, G. (1999), Asset Bubbles and Minsky Crises in East Asia: A Spatialized Minsky Approach, Department of Economics, University of California Riverside, April 1999.

Dymski, G. and R. Pollin (1992), "Hyman Minsky as Hedgehog: The Power of the Wall Street Paradigm", in S. Fazzari and D.B. Papadimitriou (eds.), *Financial Conditions and Macroeconomic Performance: Essays in Honor of Hyman P. Minsky*, Armonk, NY: ME Sharp, pp.27–61.

Frenkel, R. and M. Rapetti (2009), "A Developing Country View of the Current Global Crisis: What Should Not Be Forgotten and What Should Be Done", *Cambridge Journal of Economics*, vol.33, issue 4, pp.685–702.

Gray, P.G. and J.M. Gray (1994), "Minskian Fragility in the International Financial System", in G. Dymski and R. Pollin (eds.), *New Perspectives in Monetary Macroeconomics: Explorations in the Tradition of Hyman P. Minsky*, Ann Arbor, MI: University of Michigan Press, pp.143–167.

Kindleberger, C.P. (1978/2005), *Manias, Panics and Crashes: A History of Financial Crises*, Fifth Edition, Hoboken, NJ: Wiley.

Kindleberger, C.P. (1988), *The International Economic Order: Essays on Financial Crisis and International Public Goods*, Cambridge, MA: MIT Press.

Kindleberger, C.P. and R.Z. Aliber (1978/2011), *Manias, Panics, and Crashes: A History of Financial Crises*, Sixth Edition, Basingstoke: Palgrave Macmillan.

Kregel, J. (1998), "Yes, 'It' Did Happen Again: A Minsky Crisis Happened in Asia", *Working Paper*, Levy Economics Institute of Bard College, no.234, April 1998.

Kregel, J. (2010), "Is This the Minsky Moment for Reform of Financial Regulation?", *Working Paper*, Levy Economics Institute of Bard College, no.586, February 2010.

Kregel, J. (2013), "Political Economy Approaches to Financial Crisis: Hyman Minsky's Financial Fragility Hypothesis", in Wolfson, M.H. and G.A. Epstein (eds.), *The Handbook of Political Economy of Financial Crisis*, New York: Oxford University Press, pp.159–171.

McCulley, P. (2009), The Shadow Banking System and Hyman Minsky's Economic Journey, PIMCO Global Central Bank Focus, May 2009.

Mehrling, P. (1999), "The Vision of Hyman P. Minsky", *Journal of Economic Behavior & Organization*, vol.39, issue 2, pp.129–158.

Mehrling, P. (2022), *Money and Empire: Charles P. Kindleberger and the Dollar System*, Cambridge: Cambridge University Press.

Mehrling, P. (2023), "Minsky and Kindleberger: Fellow Traveling Theorists of National and International Financial Instability", *GEGI Study*, Global Economic Governance Initiative (GEGI), Global Development Policy Center, Boston University, no.59, March 2023.

Minsky, H.P. (1975/2008), *John Maynard Keynes*, New York: McGraw-Hill.

Minsky, H.P. (1979), "Financial Interrelations, the Balance of Payments, and the Dollar Crisis", in J.D. Aronson (ed.), *Debt and the Less Developed Countries*, Boulder, CO: Westview Press, pp.103–122.

Minsky, H.P. (1982), *Can 'It' Happen Again?* Armonk, NY: ME Sharpe.

Minsky, H.P. (1986a), "Conflict and Interdependence in A Multipolar World", *Studies in Banking and Finance*, vol.4, pp.3–22.

Minsky, H.P. (1986b/2008), *Stabilizing an Unstable Economy*, New York: McGraw-Hill.

Minsky, H.P. (1986c), "Global Consequences of Financial Deregulation", Hyman P. Minsky Archive, Bard College, 378.

Minsky, H.P. (1987), "Securitization", Hyman P. Minsky Archive, Bard College, 15.

Minsky, H.P. (1988), "Schumpeter: Finance and Evolution", Hyman P. Minsky Archive, Bard College, 314.

Minsky, H.P. (1991), "The Financial Instability Hypothesis: A Clarification", in M. Feldstein (ed.), *The Risk of Economic Crisis*, Chicago, IL: University of Chicago Press, pp.158–166.

Minsky, H.P. (1992), "The Financial Instability Hypothesis", *Working Paper*, Levy Economics Institute of Bard College, no.74, May 1992.

Nesvetailova, A. (2007), *Fragile Finance: Debt, Speculation and Crisis in the Age of Global Credit*, Basingstoke: Palgrave Macmillan.

Nesvetailova, A. (2010), "Reclaimed by the Mainstream? Hyman Minsky and the Global Credit Crunch", in D. Tavasci and J. Toporowski (eds.), *Minsky, Crisis and Development*, Basingstoke: Palgrave Macmillan, pp.90–105.

Pollin, P. (1991), "Two Theories of Money Supply Endogeneity: Some Empirical Evidence", *Journal of Post Keynesian Economics*, vol.13, issue 3, pp.366–396.

Schroeder, S.K. (2002), "A Minskian Analysis of Financial Crisis in Developing Countries", *CEPA Working Paper*, Center for Economic Policy Analysis (CEPA), New School University, 2002–09, August 2002.

Strange, S. (1986/2016), *Casino Capitalism*, Manchester: Manchester University Press.

Wolfson, M.H. (2002), "Minsky's Theory of Financial Crises in a Global Context", *Journal of Economic Issues*, vol.36, issue 2, pp.393–400.

Wray, R. (2006), "Extending Minsky's Classifications of Fragility to Government and the Open Economy", *Working Paper*, Levy Economics Institute of Bard College, no.450, May 2006.

Part II

The fundamentals of the US dollar standard system

3 The comparative advantage of the US shadow banking system in the 2000s

1 The structural shortage of global safe assets in the 2000s

As mentioned in Chapter 1 (Introduction), G-SIBs in the US and Europe increased their gross balance sheets denominated in the dollar in the 2000s before the Global Financial Crisis (GFC) of 2007–09. What facilitated global systemically important banks (G-SIBs) to expand their gross balance sheets during this period? One deep-rooted cause was a shortage of global safe assets, led by an insufficient supply of US government-guaranteed safe assets such as US Treasury securities (US Treasuries, for short) in comparison with strong demand for them since the 1990s, especially the 2000s.

On the one hand, improvements in fiscal position in major developed countries except Japan resulted in curtailing the issuance of their government securities available for safe assets in the late 1990s. In some countries, the improvement was projected to continue well, leading to the possibility of an inadequate supply of sovereign debts (Schinasi, Kramer and Smith 2001). In the US, in fiscal year 1999, government revenues exceeded spending by $123 billion, resulting in the first consecutive budget surpluses since the middle of the 1950s. The budget surpluses decreased the stock of US public debt held by the public, which was $3.6 trillion on September 30, 1999, down from its peak of $3.8 trillion a year and a half before (Fleming [2000], p.130). As such, the supply of high-quality government-guaranteed safe assets in major developed nations such as the US was relatively limited in the 2000s before the GFC (Davies 2020).

One the other hand, two structural demands stood out for explaining the insatiable need for government-guaranteed safe assets in the 2000s. First, the emergence of a distinct type of capital accumulation dominated by finance, in short, what is now widely called financialization (Epstein 2005), generated a structural demand for global safe assets from institutional investors. Financialization is essentially rooted in structural change in capital accumulation in advanced countries, starting roughly in the late 1970s or the early 1980s in developed economies, particularly the US. Why has financialization develop since then? Major advanced countries have confronted a structural problem

DOI: 10.4324/9781003733959-5

of overaccumulation due to the lack of attractive possibilities to reinvest past profits in production since the late 1960s.[1] This structural problem increasingly undermined the demand-led higher economic growth under the 'Golden Age of Capitalism' in the 1960s, which led developed countries to face a systemic shortage of domestic demand (Palley [2012], p.17). In response, major advanced nations adopted neoliberalism to revive the rate of profit at firms, which moved on an upward trend since 1982, though with cyclical downturns in the early 1990s and the early 2000s (Panitch and Ginden [2012], p.183). The revival in the rate of profit, in turn, has increasingly facilitated an accumulation of large cash balances held by large corporations. Most of their substantial cash balances, combined with households' savings, are managed largely by institutional investors. In these circumstances, institutional investors have become the dominant investable funds for high-yield safe assets over the past decades. Total financial assets of institutional investors reached $46,021 billion in 2005, of which the US accounted for $21,181 billion and the Eurozone reached $10,165 billion (CGFS (2007), p.5).

Institutional investors are mainly classified as two pools: long pools and cash pools who need to invest in safe assets (Pozsar 2011, 2014, 2015). One the one hand, the long pools are pension funds, mutual funds, hedge funds, and exchange-traded funds (ETFs), etc., who steer their cash balances to purchasing safe, long-term, and triple A-rated debt securities with relatively high-yield substitutes to lending. On the other hand, the cash pools, often called institutional cash pools, are money market mutual funds (MMMFs), insurance companies, assets managers, etc., who demand various types of safe, short-term, and liquid instruments with relatively high-yield alternatives to insured bank deposits.

Second, foreign investors, particularly foreign central banks in emerging markets and developing countries, have increased their demands for safe assets, particularly US Treasury bonds, since the late 1990s. Though depending on the country, foreign official holdings in emerging market countries are motivated primarily by a desire for a liquid and stable store of value for foreign exchange reserves, which government-guaranteed safe assets such as US Treasury bonds do well. Outstanding US Treasury securities increased from $4,080 billion in 2001 to $ 5,923 billion in 2007, in which foreign holdings rose twofold from $1,095 billion to $2,376 billion, resulting in the share of foreign owners in total holding US Treasury bonds rose from 26.85 percent to 40.12 percent between two points.[2]

All in all, these structural demands for safe assets such as US Treasury securities, in comparison with the insufficient supply of government-guaranteed safe assets, resulted in the shortage of global safe assets in the 2000s. In response, as analyzed by some studies, G-SIBs issued USD-denominated long-term and short-term safe assets through the US shadow banking system in the 2000s prior to the GFC,[3] which contributed to G-SIBs expanding their gross balance sheets in the dollar. However, few studies analyzed what determined G-SIBs, especially European banks, to denominate their gross balance sheets in the dollar, rather than the euro, in the 2000s prior to the GFC. To provide such an explanation, two important issues must be addressed in the following sections. First, it is necessary to compare the US shadow banking system to that of the Eurozone in the 2000s (Sections 2, 3 and 4). Second, it is necessary to examine the institutional differences in monetary policy on both sides of the Atlantic (Section 5).[4]

2 Shadow banking system

2.1 The development of the shadow banking system on both sides of the Atlantic

In order to supply global safe assets, G-SIBs followed the asset and liability management (ALM) strategy based on an 'originate-to-distribute' (OTD) model, in which financial intermediation is largely channeled through the shadow banking system, which was much less regulated than the traditional banking system in the 2000s prior to the GFC of 2007–09.

The shadow banking system has developed on both sides of the Atlantic since the 1990s, especially the 2000s. Many scholars and policymakers have improved the definitional framework of the shadow banking system, which is often called 'market-based finance system' or 'nonbank financial intermediation', to monitor the rise of its financial vulnerabilities at the national and international level since the GFC.[5] However, measuring the relative size of the shadow banking system is not straightforward due to (1) the heterogeneity of entities and activities, (2) the fact that shadow banking is not easy to distinguish from traditional and commercial banking, and (3) its scalability and evolving nature (Maes [2015], p.349). We make use of a broader entity-based approach which allows us to capture the growth of the shadow banking system relative to the traditional banking system.[6] Figure 3.1 illustrates that outstanding shadow banking assets had increased relative to the traditional banking assets in the US from 1990 to 2010 complied by the US Fed's flows of funds accounts.

The size of the US shadow banking system had increased since the early 1990s, especially the 2000s, prior to the GFC. The size of the shadow banking assets rose from $2,630 billion in 1990 to $26,097 billion in 2007. Though its size was smaller than the traditional banking system in the first half of the 1990s, the shadow banking assets had surpassed that of the traditional banking assets since the middle of the 1990s. Finally, the shadow banking assets reached almost twice the size of the traditional banking assets in 2007 just before the GFC.

Meanwhile, the shadow banking system in the Eurozone had also grown in the 2000s prior to the GFC. Figure 3.2 exhibits that outstanding shadow banking assets had increased compared to the traditional banking assets in

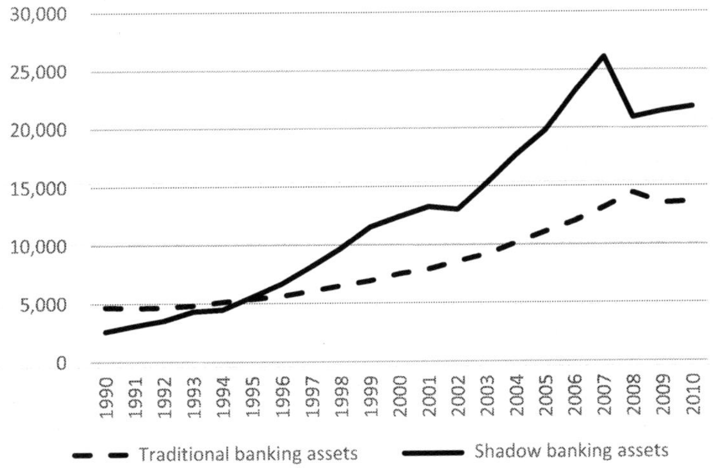

Figure 3.1 The Shadow Banking Assets Relative to the Traditional Banking Assets in the US in 1990–2010 ($ Billion; Yearly)

Sources: US flows of funds accounts of the US complied on the basis of the definition from Pozsar et al. (2010/2012), The Financial Crisis Inquiry Commission (2011), and Adrian (2017).

Notes: Traditional banking assets refer to total assets of monetary authority (L.109) and private depository institutions (L.110). Shadow banking assets contain security brokers and dealers (L.130), finance companies (L.128), issuers of asset-backed securities (L.127), money market funds (L.121), mutual funds (L.122), exchange-traded funds (L.124), and real estate investment trusts (L.129).

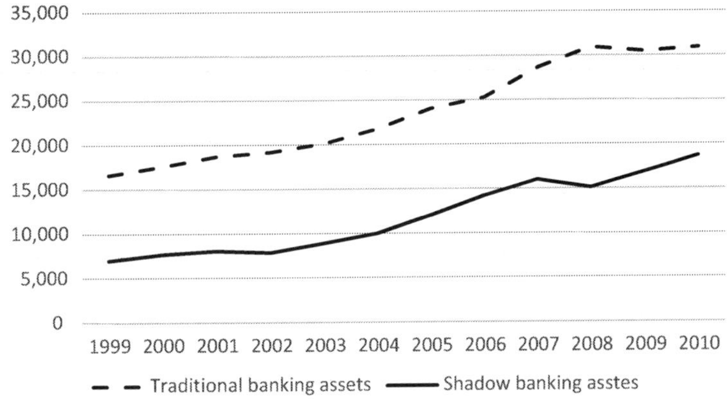

Figure 3.2 The Shadow Banking Assets Relative to the Traditional Banking Assets in the Eurozone in 1999–2010 (€ Billion; Yearly)

Sources: ECB/Eurosystem compiled on the basis of the definition from Bakk-Simon et al. (2012), and Doyle et al. (2016), and Hodula (2018).

Notes: Traditional banking assets refer to monetary financial institutions which include the central bank, other deposit-taking corporations, and money market funds (before 2005). Shadow banking assets include residual other financial intermediaries (OFIs), non-MMF investment funds, money market funds (since 2006), and financial vehicle corporations (FVCs).

the Eurozone from 1999 to 2010 compiled by the Euro area accounts of ECB/Eurosystem. The size of the shadow banking assets in the Eurozone rose from €6,988 trillion in 1999 to €16.001 in 2007, which is less than that of the traditional banking assets during the period.

Thus, the shadow banking system on both sides of the Atlantic had developed in the 2000s prior to the GFC of 2007–09.

2.2 *Financial intermediation in the shadow banking system*

Pozsar et al. (2010/2012) and Claessens et al. (2012) point out two functions of the shadow banking system that are most important economically relative to those of the traditional banking system: securitization and collateral intermediation, as represented in Figure 3.3.

On the one hand, securitization is a process that, through tranching, repackages cash flows from underlying loans and creates both long-term triple A-rated debt securities (e.g., mortgage-backed securities and asset-backed securities) and short-term liquid instruments (e.g., asset-backed commercial paper) that are perceived as safe by market participants. As we explain later, it is believed that most of processes in securitization were conducted through off-balance sheet vehicles such as special purpose vehicles (SPVs), structured investment vehicles (SIVs), and conduits established in offshore financial centers (OFCs), which are used by a handful of G-SIBs in the US and Europe including US commercial banks, US dealer banks, and European banks. As illustrated in Figure 3.3, the securitization process meets three demands from the long pools and the cash pools. First, the securitization function responds to the demand from the long pools such as hedge funds that invest their cash

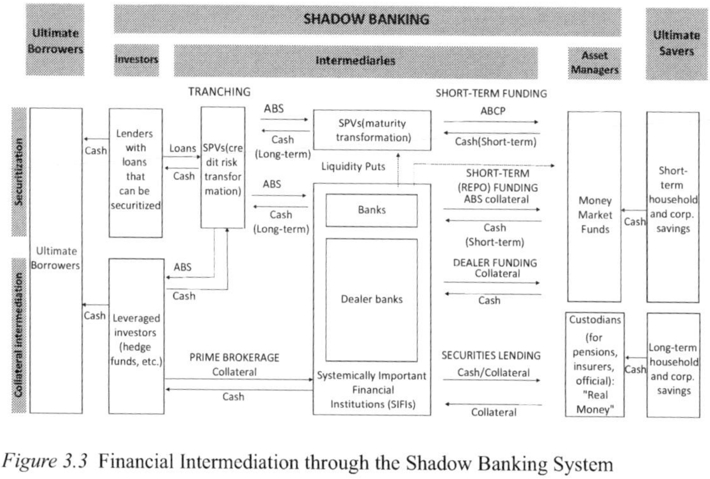

Figure 3.3 Financial Intermediation through the Shadow Banking System

Source: Reproduced from Claessens et al. (2012), p.20.

Notes: ABS = asset-backed security; ABCP = asset-backed commercial paper; SPV = special purpose vehicle.

balances into long-term triple A-rated debt securities with relatively high yield. The securitization allows off-balance sheet vehicles established by banks and dealer banks to turn illiquid assets into private-label debt securities, such as mortgage-backed securities (MBSs), asset-backed securities (ABSs), and collateralized debt obligations (CDOs), in response to the strong demand for the long-term triple A-rated debt securities from the long pools in the 2000s. Second, securitization caters to the demand from banks and dealer banks that use long-term triple A-rated debt securities with relatively high yield such as ABSs, as well as US Treasuries and US Agencies, as collateral assets for short-term wholesale borrowings in repurchase agreements (in short, repos) with the cash pools. Lastly, the securitization function responds to the demand for safe, short-term, and liquid safe assets with relatively high yields such as asset-backed commercial papers (ABCPs) from the cash pools, often called institutional cash pools (Pozsar 2011) and Pozsar and Singh (2011).

Another important function of the shadow banking system is collateral intermediation that supports a wide range of financial transactions, including demands from secured funding such as repos, securities lending, and derivatives. Collateral intermediation is essential for repos. Repos are essentially a pair of transactions between two entities: an agreement to buy security now (the opening leg of the repo) in exchange for providing cash, combined with an agreement to sell back the same security in the future at a maturity price (the closing leg of the repo). Security acts as a collateral asset, which mitigates the buyer's exposure to counterparty credit risk. In this case, repos can be recognized as safe, short-term, and collateral-backed funding. As demonstrated in Figure 3.3, dealer banks (dealers, for short, or often called broker-dealers or securities dealers), central subsidiaries of G-SIBs, play pivotal roles in collateral intermediation between the long pools and the cash pools by simultaneously transferring cash and collaterals, which involves the receipt and supply of primary collateral assets and the reuse of collateral (i.e., rehypothecation), making the shadow banking system collateral-intensive.

2.3 The development of the global shadow banking system

As the G-SIBs pursued global strategies based on the OTD model, financial intermediation through the shadow banking system flowed across borders. On the liability side, G-SIBs depended on short-term dollar borrowings. In particular, European banks came to rely heavily on short-term dollar borrowings, of which US Money Market Mutual Funds (MMMFs) were key providers in the run-up to the financial crisis (Baba et al. [2009], p.67). Also, US dealer banks relied extensively on short-term dollar funding through the globally integrated repo market before the financial crisis, as can be seen in the following quotation from the Survey of Current Business by the US Bureau of Economic Analysis (BEA):

> Liabilities of U.S. securities brokers (dealer banks: author) increased $32.7 billion in 2006, compared with an increase of $13.0 billion in 2005. The increase was largely in the form of repurchase agreements with nonbanks in the United Kingdom
>
> (Bach [2007], p.42)

On the asset side, G-SIBs, especially European banks, used their short-term dollar borrowing for purchasing long-term, safe, and triple A-rated assets, issued by securitization, on US borrowers such as subprime mortgage debtors.

Overall, G-SIBs borrowed short-term dollar funds, in part, from the US, and then lent part of it back to invest in private long-term, safe, and triple A-rated assets in the US, which are actually 'round tripping' transactions, as shown by He and McCauley (2012) and Shin (2012). By pursuing the round-tripping transactions under the global ALM strategies in the global shadow banking system, G-SIBs had expanded their USD-denominated gross balance sheets in the 2000s before the GFC.

3 The fuller development of the US shadow banking system in the 2000s

3.1 Securitization and collateral intermediation in the US

Now we turn to the next question: What led G-SIBs, particularly European banks, to denominate their gross balance sheets across the Atlantic in the dollar in the 2000s, despite the creation of the euro? To answer, the following sections (Sections 3 and 4) discuss whether or not the shadow banking system on both sides of the Atlantic could adequately fulfill its two important functions, i.e., securitization and collateral intermediation in the 2000s before the Global Financial Crisis (GFC) of 2007–09.

On one hand, securitization has played an important role in US financial markets. Securitization in the US dated back to the early 1970s, when government-sponsored entities (GSEs) pooled mortgage assets and issued mortgage-backed securities (MBSs) against the mortgage assets pool. The Government National Mortgage Association, called Ginnie Mae, pooled mortgage loans and sold MBSs against their pool. The Federal Home Loan Mortgage Corporation (Freddie Mac) and the Federal National Mortgage Association (Fannie Mae) followed Ginnie Mae in securitizing mortgages in the early 1980s (FDIC 2006). The securitization of these GSEs facilitated the issuance of new classes of debt securities, commonly referred to as US Agency securities (US Agencies, for short), which are explicitly guaranteed or implicitly supported by US government (Isaac and Reed, Jr 2017). As such, US Agencies are recognized by market participants almost as safe as US Treasuries.

GSEs' mortgage securitizations were followed by private securitization activity since the 1990s. Dealer banks and commercial banks have begun to move some mortgage assets off their on-balance sheets into legal entities generically known as off-balance sheet vehicles, thereby creating private-label and triple A-rated debt securities denominated in the dollar, including MBSs, ABSs, and CDOs which were perceived by US domestic and foreign investors almost as safe as US Treasuries and US Agencies. The global issuance of ABSs reached $17.6 trillion between 1999 and 2008, and more than two-thirds (67.9 percent) of the global issuance of ABSs was by issuers located in the US, most of which were denominated in US dollar (99.5 percent) (ECB [2009], p.32). In short, the fuller development of securitization in the US resulted in the issuing of US private-label debt securities such as MBSs, ABSs, and CDOs with relatively higher returns that were almost as safe as US Treasuries and US Agencies.

On the other hand, the well functioning of collateral intermediation is critical for US repo markets, which have represented the fastest growing component of short-term wholesale funding for banks and nonbank financial institutions (NBFIs) since the 1970s. The institutional developments in contracting conventions in US repo markets contributed to the repo markets growing by leaps and bounds since the 1980s. First, the Bankruptcy Amendments and Federal Judgeship Act of 1984 exempted repos on US Treasuries and US Agencies from the application of automatic stay. Second, the Bankruptcy Abuse Prevention and Consumer Protection Act of 2005 expanded the definition of repos to include mortgage loans, mortgage-related securities, or interest from mortgage loans or mortgage securities, and all mortgage-related repo securities become exempt from the application of automatic stay (Garbade 2006; Acharya and Öncü 2010, 2014).[7]

The US repo markets can be split into two main segments: bilateral repo market and tri-party market (Figure 3.4).

First, the bilateral repo market has investors and collateral providers directly exchanging cash and securities as collateral assets. Typically, bilateral repo transactions are preferred when market participants want to interact directly with each other or if specific collateral is requested. Second, the tri-party repo market is generally used to finance general collateral (GC), a basket of nonspecific government securities. In addition, there is the general collateral finance (GCF) repo service introduced in 1998 by the Fixed Income Clearing Corporation (FICC), a central counterparty (CCP). The GCF repo is

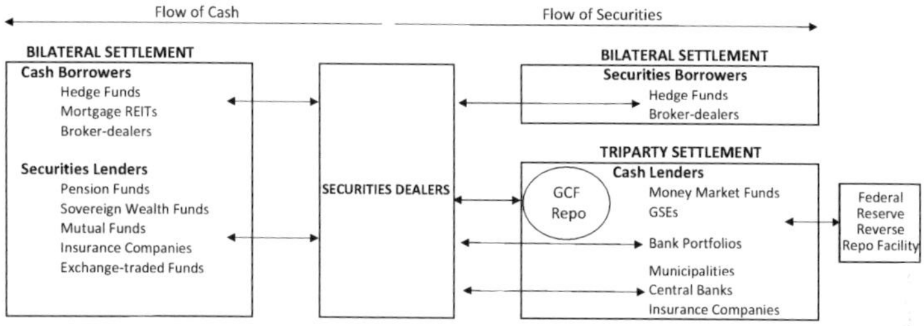

Figure 3.4 Key Repo Market Participants

Source: Reproduced from Baklanova, Dalton and Tompaidis (2017), Figure 1, p.2.

Notes: REITs = real estate investment trusts; GSEs = government-sponsored enterprises; GCF = general collateral financing repo service.

originally designed to be used among dealer banks, in which the FICC interposes itself as the legal counterparty to cash providers and collateral providers in repo transactions (Agueci et al. 2014).[8] It has been recognized in qualitative and anecdotal terms that US Treasury securities have played a dominant role as collateral assets in US repo markets, whereas US Agencies, all types of private-label MBSs, all types of ABSs, and tranches of structured products have also been used as collateral since the last half of the 1990s (Acharya and Öncü [2010], p.330).

Borrowing in the US repo market was also less costly than in the Eurozone. Because repo rates were far below deposit rates in the US, repo borrowing was more attractive. The average spread for the three-month maturity between the interbank rate and the GC repo rate in the US was 21 basis points between June 2001 and June 2002, compared to 9 basis points in the Eurozone (ECB [2002], p.61). Total US repo activity reached its peak in the 2000s before the 2007–09 financial crisis, ranging from $5 to $10 trillion (Baklanova, Copeland and McCaughrin [2015], p.1). As such, US repo markets became "the largest and most liquid short-term funding markets in the world" (OFR [2024], p.63).[9]

Overall, the substantial growth of securitization and collateral intermediation in the US contributed to the fuller development of the US shadow banking system in the 2000s prior to the GFC.

3.2 *The US shadow banking system and offshore financial centers*

Notably, G-SIBs expanded their USD-denominated gross balance sheets in the US shadow banking system, some of which were closely linked to offshore financial centers (OFCs), especially the United Kingdom (UK) and Caribbean financial centers in the 2000s. The US shadow banking system and OFCs nexus is recognized in the following quotation from the Survey of Current Business published by the US Bureau of Economic Analysis (BEA):

> (In 2004: author), these large outflows (US external banking assets: author) from US banks and US securities brokers (dealer banks: author) were nearly matched by large inflows (US external banking liabilities: author) to US banks and US securities brokers; most of the inflows and outflows were channeled through the United Kingdom and the Caribbean.
>
> (Bach [2005], p.40)

The growth of the round-tripping banking flows between the US shadow banking system and OFCs can also be demonstrated in the linkage of international dollar banking in the 2000s just before the GFC. As of the second quarter in 2007, the two largest gross banking linkages denominated in the dollar, between the US and the UK, and the US and Caribbean financial centers, were \$3.5 trillion and \$3.3 trillion, respectively, implying that G-SIBs expanded their USD-denominated gross balance sheets interlinking with OFCs such as the UK and Caribbean financial centers (McGuire and Tarashev [2007], p.51).

OFCs are roughly divided into two components in terms of financial activities and transactions.[10] The first is the Eurocurrency market, which is more or less not subject to domestic financial regulation. London has been the largest Eurodollar market to play a role in global financial intermediation, transferring surplus dollars between lenders and borrowers involving US financial institutions, non-US banks, institutional investors, large multinationals and central banks, etc.[11] The second is secrecy jurisdictions called tax havens, with lax financial regulation and light tax supervision. For instance, Caribbean financial centers are tax havens functioning as booking centers for off-balance vehicles established by G-SIBs.

What factors led G-SIBs to partly expand their gross balance sheets denominated in the dollar through OFCs? One of the major factors was avoiding domestic financial regulation and maximizing tax avoidance in OFCs, in which G-SIBs established off-balance sheet vehicles such as special purpose vehicles (SPVs), structured investment vehicles (SIVs), and conduits. The Cayman Islands attracted G-SIBs to use off-balance sheet vehicles for their activities for the US shadow banking system in the 2000s before the GFC. First, the Cayman Islands are free of financial regulations. According to Anthony Travers who supported establishing the Cayman Islands as OFC, "the responsibility of the Cayman government was managed by avoiding the concept of prudential regulation" (Shaxson [2019], p.153). Second, the Cayman Islands have zero-tax status. Cayman's SPVs "are entitled to a complete tax holiday for 20 years, with the possibility of a 10-year extension on offshore earnings" (Bryan, Rafferty and Wigan [2016], p.952). These features of the Cayman Islands contributed to G-SIBs' activities in the US shadow banking being partly incorporated in the Islands.[12] In short, the US shadow banking system was intimately linked to OFCs in the 2000s.

Along with the rising of the US shadow banking system-OFCs nexus, G-SIBs have intensively used these regions for facilitating their securitization activity and collateral intermediation in the US in the 2000s before the financial crisis. On the one hand, securitization across the borders has increasingly become an important area of cross-border finance (Schwarcz 2002). Cross-border securitization consists of several stages designed and executed in different countries to form a desired financial intermediation scheme. Frankel (1998) explains the structure of cross-border securitization as analogous with offshoring production by large multinationals. As large US multinationals pursue offshoring in production, they no longer assume that their manufacturing, marketing, or purchasing should be located exclusively in the US. Instead, they establish various parts of their operations in different countries. Analogous with the offshoring in US multinationals, cross-border securitization depends on (1) opportunities to create an inventory of financial assets by originating, buying, or selling; (2) optimal regulation and tax laws; (3) various risks and their levels; and (4) absence or presence of an institutional or legal infrastructure (Frankel 1998, p.264).[13] To fulfill the securitization activity, G-SIBs register many off-balance sheet vehicles such SPVs, SIVs, and conduits in OFCs. Frankel (1998) notes that SPVs in London and other OFCs play a critical role in cross-border securitization activities as below:

> Where such barriers exist, financial assets originated in one country are often structured in another country. For example, London is the location of major sponsors that package assets originated in other countries and distribute the securities backed by these assets. The securities are structured to meet the demands of investors in particular markets…The special purpose vehicles used to securitize these assets, however, are often located not in London but in other financial centers, such as the Channel Islands.
>
> (p.266; underlines are by author)

As such, a fraction of processes in securitization activity in the US shadow banking system was conducted through OFCs.[14]

Cross-border collateral intermediation has, on the other hand, been partly conducted through the US repo markets that have interconnected with the Eurodollar market in London, which plays the role of a global financial intermediary that recycles substantial amounts of surplus Eurodollars. As McGuire (2004) points out, London had gone through a shift in the recycling of Eurodollars since the middle of the 1990s. Until the mid-1990s, most of the Eurodollars in London had been recycled in the interbank market. But surplus Eurodollars in London from the banking sector were primarily used to finance nonbank borrowers such as dealer banks, hedge funds, and other nonbank financial firms in the US which have partly depended on Eurodollar borrowings from banks in London to increase leverage through repos (McGuire 2004, pp.74–76). Thus, the Eurodollar market in London recycled a portion of the abundant global dollar funds that allowed G-SIBs to borrow short-term dollar funds in the shadow banking system.

Overall, the deeper integration of the US shadow banking system and OFCs reinforced the fuller development of the US shadow banking system in the 2000s before the GFC.

4 The underdevelopment of the shadow banking system in the Eurozone in the 2000s

Because the issuance of government bonds in the Eurozone grew at a slower pace than the European repo market, there was a rising demand for alternative, privately created debt securities as collateral assets in the 2000s prior to the financial crisis (ECB 2006). In this respect, there was also a shortage of safe assets denominated in the euro within the Eurozone in the 2000s. Were securitization and collateral intermediation in the Eurozone capable of responding to the shortage of euro-denominated safe assets?

The introduction of the euro, together with increased demand from institutional investors and financial innovations, encouraged the development of securitization in the Eurozone (Prati and Schinasi [1997], p.264; Altunbas, Gambacorta and Marqués [2007], p.10). New issuance of securitized assets in the European Union (EU) increased in the 2000s and peaked in 2008. For example, new issuance of securitized assets such as residential mortgage-backed securities (RMBSs) in the European Union rose from around €50 billion in 2000 to more than €700 billion in 2008 (Kozak and Teplova [2012], Figure 3, p.35).[15]

However, securitization activity was lower in the Eurozone than in the US before the financial crisis. Securitized issuance, for instance, amounted to €462 billion, compared with $1.7 trillion in the US, or around 5 percent and 12 percent of GDP, respectively (Bakk-Simon et al. [2012], p.13). The underdevelopment of securitization in the Eurozone was mainly due to three factors. First, European banks have retained the majority of securitized assets on their gross balance sheets, rather than offloading the assets to other investors.[16] Second, the development of securitization in the Eurozone remained variable across countries and sectors (Altunbas, Gambacorta and Marqués [2007], p.11). Finally, institutional differences in lending criteria, banking institutions, rating standards, and default laws in the course of securitization remain important (Hakkarainen [2014], p.3). The weaknesses of securitization in the Eurozone relative to the US impeded the ability of European banks to make privately created debt securities denominated in the euro, in response to the shortage of euro-denominated safe assets in the Eurozone in the 2000s.[17]

With respect to collateral intermediation in the Eurozone, institutional developments in wholesale funding were expected to spur growth of the Eurozone-wide repo market in the 2000s.[18] Even though the introduction of the euro induced the expansion of wholesale financial markets, encouraging the unsecured money market and government bond markets to be closely integrated, there remained several areas that were insufficiently integrated (Schinasi and Teixeira [2006], p.3). As Gabor and Ban (2015) suggested, "[I]n an area characterized by a single currency, old rules and market architectures may be unsuited to the task and become instead the main obstacles to the attainment of a higher degree of efficiency" (p.623). According to the Giovannini Group (1999), "The repo market is a perfect illustration of this problem" (p.1). To support establishment of a Eurozone-wide repo market, the Eurozone initiated a series of institutional reforms through 'a private-public joint venture' prior to the GFC (Gabor 2016a). Specifically, the European Commission launched the Financial Services Action Plan (FSAP) in 1999, which was a set of legislative-regulatory harmonization policies aimed at tackling the last remaining obstacles to the integration of the wholesale market. Above all, the FSAP's legislative agenda included the planned adoption of new directives on the cross-border use of collateral and market manipulation (ECB [2012], p.37). Additionally, from the outset, the ECB accepted a broader range of collateral assets in its open market operations than other central banks in advanced countries, thus promoting the development of Eurozone-wide repo markets (Eichengreen [1997], p.18; Prati and Schinasi [1997], p.276; Gabor [2016b], pp.931–932). In this connection, the ECB created a euro general collateral (GC) basket called 'Euro GC Polling' that included all Economic and Monetary Union government bonds in the same liquidity category, encouraging private repo market activity in the Eurozone. This development facilitated repo transactions via a central counterparty (CCP) and offered an automated cross-border collateral management system allowing banks to reuse GC collateral as well as pledging collateral with the ECB (Hördahl and King [2008], p.48). As a result, the outstanding volume in the European repo market (repo plus reverse repo positions) increased from €1,863 billion in June 2001 to €6,775 billion in June 2007.[19] Thus, Eurozone-wide repo markets became an important source of short-term euro funding for European banks in the 2000s prior to the GFC of 2007–09.

Nevertheless, similar to the underdevelopment of securitization, significant barriers and constraints on the development of Eurozone-wide collateral intermediation remained in the 2000s. First, although the ECB accepted a broader range of collateral assets through its open market operations, most collateral in private repo markets in the Eurozone consisted of government bonds. According to average collateral usage during 2006 in primary and secondary funding, ECB collateral consisted mainly of central government bonds (22.50 percent), uncovered (31.50 percent) and covered bank bonds

(13.20 percent), and ABSs (12.10 percent). By contrast, collateral asset usage of privately produced debt securities in the private repo market in the European Union reached only 15.8 percent, whereas central government bonds accounted for 84.2 percent in 2006 (Ewehart and Tapking [2008], p.54). Second, the ECB became more selective about government bonds in the Eurozone used as eligible collateral in its refinancing operations after December 2005. The ECB stipulated that government bonds must have a single A-rating, or better, from at least one of three rating agencies suggested (Financial Times, November 9, 2005, as Cohen [2011], p.84). Finally, many barriers to efficient cross-border securities settlement remained unaddressed, which meant that Europe could not establish an integrated wholesale funding market (ECB 2014; ICMA 2014). The insufficient integration and fragmented infrastructure for European securities settlement resulted in a higher cost of clearing and settlement across borders in the European Union compared to US and domestic EU clearing and settlement. Cross-border costs in the European Union range from €19.5 to €35.0, whereas domestic EU costs range from €0.35 to €3.43, and US costs range from €0.10 to €2.90 (ECB [2007], p.6). Taken together, the lower growth of securitization and collateral intermediation within the Eurozone than those of the US led to the underdevelopment of the shadow banking system in the Eurozone in the 2000s prior to the GFC.

Overall, it follows from the comparative analysis of the shadow banking system on both sides of the Atlantic that the US shadow banking system had an advantage over the one in the Eurozone in the 2000s before the GFC.

5 The evolution of US Fed policy

5.1 The function of lender of last resort

As already noted, the US shadow banking system has expanded greatly since the 1990s. The development of the shadow banking system contributed to shadow financial intermediation becoming longer lasting and more variegated in the US compared to the traditional commercial banking system. Thus, the interconnectedness between various financial institutions, particularly the nexus between banks and nonbank financial institutions (NBFIs), rose commensurately.[20] The increase in the interconnectedness within the shadow banking system resulted in the buildup of systemic risk, arising from bank failure and default, which has led to the recurrence of financial crises.

The recurrence of crises has raised the need for a central bank to function as a lender of last resort (LLR) in order to counter financial distress. Commercial banks were able to access the central bank's discount window and deposit insurance in time of financial crisis, but NBFIs within the US shadow banking system were not able to access these liquidity backstops. In essence, the LLR policy rule is that the central bank should lend freely at penalty rates against good collateral in order to save solvent but temporarily illiquid banks (first recognized by Walter Bagehot in the second half of the 19th century.) Along with the development of the shadow banking system, it became necessary for the central bank to assume the function of the LLR in the course of counter-cyclical monetary policy, with the aim of rescuing not only commercial banks but also NBFIs faced with systemic risk.

The US Fed has expanded the scope of the LLR to support the development of US shadow banking system since the 1990s. Similarly, it was necessary for the European Central Bank (ECB) to play the role of the LLR in the Eurozone in view of the rapid evolution of the European Monetary Union (EMU) in the 1990s, which relied on European financial markets becoming more liquid and securitization developing further (Folkerts-Landau and Garber [1992], p.31). In short, it became crucial for both the Fed and the ECB to play the role of the LLR as the shadow banking system developed on both sides of the Atlantic. But their respective roles unfolded quite differently in the 2000s.

The US Fed understands fully that the function of the LLR goes beyond stabilizing US commercial banks (Folkerts-Landau and Garber [1992], p.25). Furthermore, the Fed comprehends implicitly its responsibility for playing the role of 'international lender of last resort' for non-US banks. Since the Mexico currency crisis of 1982, the US Fed has already played the role of the international LLR.[21] As we detail in Chapter 6.1, at the time of the GFC of 2007–09, the Fed provided a massive amount of LLR loans to foreign financial institutions, especially European banks, which were experiencing severe dollar funding shortages. Thus, the function of LLR delivered by the US Fed was the ability to backstop not only for US financial institutions but also for non-US financial institutions faced with financial failure.

Consider now the impact of the institutional framework of the Eurosystem on the ability of the ECB to act fully as LLR in the Eurozone. The Maastricht Treaty signed in 1992, which was the blueprint for advancing toward the EMU, provided the legal basis for the European System of Central Banks (ESCB), which comprises the ECB and the national central banks (NCBs) of member states of the EU. The Eurosystem stands for a subset of the ESCB that comprises the ECB and the NCBs of countries that have adopted the euro (Gerdesmeier, Mongelli and Roffia [2007], p.8). The basic tasks of the Eurosystem include implementation of monetary policy, conducting foreign exchange operations, holding and managing the official foreign reserves, and promoting the smooth operation of payment systems (Article 105.2 of the Maastricht Treaty). Although the institutional framework of the Eurosystem appears to be similar to other central banks in advanced countries, monetary policy in the Eurosystem is decentralized. Specifically, while monetary policy is entrusted to the ECB, the responsibility for banking supervision is still in the hands of the NCBs (Moutot, Jung and Mongelli [2008], pp.18–19). This decentralized structure in monetary policy raises the concern that the ECB could not sufficiently function as the LLR in times of crisis. Instead, the Eurosystem provided emergency liquidity assistance (ELA), which was summed up as follows by the European Central Bank (1999):

> Co-ordination mechanisms are primarily called for within the Eurosystem. This is the case for emergency liquidity assistance (ELA), which embraces the support given by central banks in exceptional circumstances and on a case-by-case basis to temporarily illiquid institutions and markets. At the outset, it is necessary to stress that the importance of ELA should not be overemphasized…The main guiding principle is that the competent NCB (national central bank: author) takes the decision concerning the provision of ELA to an institution operating in its jurisdiction. This would take place under the responsibility and at the cost of the NCB in question.
>
> (p.98)

As the quotation explains, although the advance of the ELA could be considered an exceptional provision of central bank liquidity to individual banks facing temporary liquidity problems that are solvent and have good collateral, it is far from clear that the ECB could advance ELA in the face of financial crisis. This unclear stance of the central bank regarding the provision of liquidity is called 'constructive ambiguity'. The stance is based on the concern that overly generous LLR assistance might generate moral hazard among financial institutions, allowing them to encourage excessive leverage and risk-taking (IMF [2014], p.102). In order to avoid moral hazard, policymakers introduced ambiguity in the implementation of the LLR.

So, could the ECB play the role of the LLR in the face of a Eurozone-wide financial crisis? On the one hand, Papadoa-Schioppa (2000) stressed that Articles 105.5 and 105.6 of the Maastricht Treaty seem to ensure that 'competent authorities' pursue a smooth interplay between monetary policy and supervisory responsibilities. If these articles were followed fully, the concern about the separation of monetary policy from banking supervisory responsibilities would disappear. Hence, the procedure defined by the Maastricht Treaty could be interpreted as a 'last resort clause', which enables the ECB to play the role of the LLR (Papadoa-Schioppa [2000], pp.17–18). On the other hand, Aglietta (2000) insisted that the Maastricht Treaty gives the ECB only a limited role to counter Eurozone-wide systemic risk. Although the possible contribution of the ECB to financial stability is mentioned in Articles 105.5 and 105.6, policies toward this purpose that were supposed to be implemented by competent authorities were not defined. Thus, the LLR function was not clearly identified in the Eurosystem (Aglietta [2000], p.47).

Which view was conceivable? As noted, responsibility for ELA lies with the NCBs, not the ECB. Any costs and risks arising from ELA operations are incurred by the NCBs themselves.[22] Due to this flaw in the provision of ELA, the ECB was forced to operate its monetary policy by cutting short-term interest rates and deploying its regular refinancing operations (rather than the ELA) as it sought to support commercial banks in the course of the subprime mortgage crisis in 2007 and until the GFC of 2008 (Herr [2014], p.70). Furthermore, the mechanism of the ELA as the LLR, as well as a series of monetary policies by the ECB, proved dysfunctional in countering the Eurozone debt crisis in 2011–13, thus causing serious damage to European banks. Based on this analysis, the ambiguity of the ECB's stance regarding the function of the LLR could be considered destructive rather than constructive.

Therefore, it is clear that the US Fed can be expected to intervene forcefully to rescue G-SIBs, including European banks, when they face trouble related to the shadow banking system. In contrast, the ECB has a major institutional flaw in delivering the role of LLR fully, although it is able to make decisions on ELA.

5.2 The US Fed 'too-big-to-fail' policy

As previously noted, the essential policy rule of the LLR is that the central bank should lend freely at penalty rates against good collateral in order to save solvent but temporarily illiquid banks. But the US Fed has increasingly lent to insolvent large banks of doubtful soundness, particularly when such large banks were judged as 'too-big-to-fail' (TBTF). The Fed and the US government have adopted the doctrine of the TBTF since the 1980s, which goes far beyond the function of the LLR. Paul Volker, probably the most powerful chairman of the Fed during the last several decades, introduced the TBTF policy in the face of the Mexico crisis and the bankruptcy of Continental Illinois at the beginning of the 1980s (Mallaby [2016], p.301). The TBTF policy is based on the belief that the failure of large banks has a negative impact on the financial system. The central bank and the government should do whatever it takes to prevent this negative impact, even if a financial bailout must be paid by the taxpayers. Although the TBTF policy could indeed rescue the financial system, it is inevitable that the TBTF policy would give Wall Street financial institutions and large European banks implicit protection of their USD-denominated assets by US policymakers in the face of financial distress (Obstfeld [2009], p.11). Large European banks and US banks enjoyed higher ex ante safety net benefits through the TBTF policy in 2003–08 (Carbo-Valverde, Kane and Rodriguez-Fernandez 2011). The de facto insurance offered through the TBTF policy could allow banks to obtain cheaper funding, thus increasing leverage on the liability side, and to engage in riskier activities on the asset side (IMF [2014], p.103). Hence, it seems safe to infer that the TBTF policy offers to G-SIBs (including European banks) the implicit certainty that their dollar assets in the US shadow banking system would be supported by US policymakers in the face of financial crisis.

5.3 The 'Greenspan put'

In addition, the US Fed under the leadership of Alan Greenspan, chairman of the Federal Reserve from 1987 to 2006, executed a peculiar monetary policy in the 2000s. The Fed cut short-term federal funds (FF) rates aggressively after the 1998 collapse of Long-Term Capital Management, a highly leveraged hedge fund, and the burst of the technology bubble in 2000, aiming to prevent deflation.[23] Immediately after the burst of the technology bubble, the Fed cut the FF rate by 50 basis points in early January 2001, and then eased intermittently, bringing it down to 0.98 percent in December 2003.[24] This is an example of what came to be known as the 'Greenspan put', namely, that the Fed would cut the FF rates sharply after the burst of a bubble. O'Driscoll (2009) and Buttonwood (2017) noted that the Greenspan put can be regarded as "the asymmetric" monetary policy (O'Driscoll [2009], p.179). The Fed would not stop the asset bubble because it professes not to know when financial markets are in bubble territory. The Fed is certain to cut the FF rate drastically to prevent deflation when the markets fall too far.[25] Greenspan (2002, pp.8–9) stated the following:

> [T]he Federal Reserve has focused on policies that would, as I testified before the Congress in 1999, "… mitigate the fallout [of an asset bubble] when it occurs and, hopefully, ease the transition to the next expansion."

The Federal Open Market Committee chose to embark on an aggressive course of monetary easing two years ago once it became apparent that a variety of forces, including the slump in household wealth that resulted from the decline in stock prices, were restraining inflation pressures and economic activity. Wall Street financial institutions welcomed the Greenspan put "because it meant that he would not raise interest rates preemptively to choke off a boom" (Johnson and Kwak [2010], pp.101–102). It was likely that the Greenspan put would trigger a new asset bubble, thus reviving financial profits of G-SIBs, including Wall Street financial institutions and European banks.

In summary, the LLR and the TBTF strategy gave G-SIBs implicit assurance that their USD-denominated assets would be protected by US policymakers in the face of financial distress. Meanwhile, the Greenspan put would trigger the next asset bubble, thus reviving financial profits of G-SIBs. To state it differently, the evolution of the US Fed monetary policy starting with the international LLR reinforced the comparative advantage of the US shadow banking system compared to the less developed shadow banking system of the Eurozone.

Therefore, it can be proposed that the comparative advantage of the US shadow banking system compared to the less developed shadow banking system of the Eurozone encouraged G-SIBs, especially European banks, to denominate their gross balance sheets in the dollar, rather than the euro, in the 2000s before the GFC of 2007–09.[26]

6 The US dollar's dominance in the shadow banking system in the 2000s

The expansion of gross balance sheets denominated in the dollar at G-SIBs, in turn, led to strong demand for USD-denominated long-term, privately debt securities and short-term liquid financial instruments created by G-SIBs in the US shadow banking system. Several factors led to this development.

First, USD-denominated long-term ABS issuances increased in an unprecedented fashion. The share of the dollar in ABS issuance rose from around 65 percent in 1999 to 75–80 percent on the eve of the financial crisis, while the share of the euro increased gradually from around 15 percent to about 20 percent during the same period (ECB [2011b], p.52, Chart 25). In addition, it is likely that the dominant position of the dollar in credit default swaps (CDSs) supported the prominence of USD-denominated ABS issues. G-SIBs bought large amounts of CDSs on ABSs and Collateralized Debt Obligations (CDOs) written by insurance companies in order to hedge credit risk associated with the underlying assets. According to the currency breakdown of credit derivatives from May 1 to July 31, 2010, the percentage of the dollar in total transactions was 63 percent, while its share reached 57 percent in total notional size. Meanwhile, the share of the euro was 35 percent and 42 percent, respectively, although these data were after the global financial crisis of 2008 (Chen et al. [2011, p.7, Table 1). Second, USD-denominated short-term financial instruments, such as ABCPs, grew rapidly in the 2000s and prior to the GFC. In total, with respect to outstanding ABCPs by funding currency as of January 2007, $714 billion out of $969 billion (or 73.7 percent) were denominated in dollars, and only $219 billion (or 22.6 percent) in euros.[27] Third, the dollar played the dominant role as collateral asset in the global repo market in the 2000s. There was no published official data of collateral category before the GFC in the 2000s. Instead, judging by the liabilities and the equity of the US domestic economy and the rest of the world in June 2007, foreign holdings of treasury bonds were the largest proportion of the amount outstanding (45 percent). The share of agency bonds, corporate bonds (non-asset-backed), and corporate ABS + ABCP reached 21 percent, 25 percent, and 22 percent, respectively (Beltran, Pounder and Thomas [2008], p.24, Table 3). Taking into account the higher share of foreigners in the holdings of US debt securities, a broad range of US debt securities was used as collateral assets in the global repo market in the 2000s and prior to the GFC. Lastly, the dominant position of the dollar in the foreign exchange (FX) swaps market allowed European banks to borrow massively in dollars. When non-US banks raise US dollar borrowings through secured transactions, they often use FX swaps to exchange domestic currency for dollars. For example, European banks would buy dollars by selling euros for dollars in the spot exchange market and then sell dollars to buy back euros in the forward exchange market. These transactions can be considered collateralized short-term dollar borrowing, due to the funding of dollar acquisitions by providing domestic currency—i.e., euros (Ando 2012). According to the use of US dollars and euros in European foreign exchange markets in April 2007, several European currencies—such as the Danish krone, the Norwegian krone, the Polish zloty, and the Swedish krona—traded more heavily in euros than in dollars in the spot market. In contrast, FX swap markets in Europe traded more heavily in dollars (McCauley [2012], p.99). Thus, G-SIBs, especially European banks, tend to rely on FX swaps to obtain dollars against euros and other European currencies. All in all, the strong demand for long-term private-label US debt securities (e.g., MBSs, ABSs, and CDOs) and short-term US financial instruments (e.g., repos, ABCPs, and FX swaps) in the US shadow banking system contributed to the US dollar's dominance in the 2000s.

Accordingly, it is suggested that the comparative advantage of the US shadow banking system interlinking with OFCs over the one in the Eurozone allowed G-SIBs to denominate their gross balance sheets in the dollar, rather than the euro, in the 2000s. Hence, the dollar's dominance in the shadow banking system enabled its revived dominance in the 2000s prior to the GFC of 2007–09.

Notes

1 Brenner (2002); Foster and Magdoff (2009); Harvey (2010); McNally (2011); Hossein-zadeh (2014); Chesnais (2016).
2 Own estimations on Board of Governors of the Federal Reserve System, Flow of funds of the US.
3 For example, Caballero (2006); Gorton and Muir (2015).
4 Most of the material in Sections 2–6 of Chapter 3 were drawn on Tokunaga and Epstein (2018) and Tokunaga (2019).
5 FSB (2015, 2019); Patalano and Roulet (2020); Aramonte, Schrimpf and Shin (2021/2022).
6 The definitions of the shadow banking system are mainly divided into the entity that carries on shadow banking activities (the entity-based approach) which we use and the activities that the entity carries on (the activity-based approach) (Hodula 2018).
7 In addition, Menand (2022) points out that the amendment to Section 13 (3) of the Federal Reserve Act in 1991, in which US Congress loosened restrictions on the US Fed's emergency lending ability for backstopping dealer banks in the face of financial panic, made it easier for dealers to fund themselves using repos (p.112).
8 In addition, 'sponsored repo' has grown since the late 2010s. In this transaction, a dealer sponsors nondealer counterparties (i.e., sponsored member) without the requirements of full membership of the clearing house—typically a hedge fund or money market fund—onto the FICC-cleared repo platform. In the meantime, the advantage of sponsored repo for banks and dealer banks is to have no balance sheet cost (Metrick and Tarullo 2021).
9 RepoWatch is a financial blog on the internet which has focused on the development of repurchase agreements since 2011. See https://repowatch.org/.
10 The discussion is based on pioneering studies on offshore financial markets. See Hampton and Abbot (1999); Dixon (2001); Palan (2003); Sharman (2006); Palan, Murphy and Chavagneus (2010); Shaxson (2011); Urry (2014).

11 The heterodox economists' arguments of the important role of the UK as OFCs in modern global finance are mainly clarified into two views. For one thing, many scholars suggest the concept of 'new British Empire', in which the UK plays a role of financial intermediation in global capital flows (Palan, Murphy and Chavagneus 2010; Shaxson 2011, 2019; Talani 2012; Norfield 2016). Specifically, the UK dependencies (Bermuda, BVI, Cayman, Jersey, Guernsey, etc.), but also its former colonies such as Cyprus, Hong Kong, and Singapore, form a kind of new British Empire in global financial flows, which is centered on the City of London. For another thing, some researchers provide 'the Anglo-American approach', in which the development of Eurodollar markets in London originating in the late 1950s, combined with the expansion of international banking by US banks, was a fundamental feature for shaping the transatlantic financial integration (i.e., NY-LON) (Wójcik 2013; Fichtner 2016; Green 2016). Both views must contribute to open new avenues for explaining the critical role of the OFCs in the unregulated global capital flows since the 1970s.

12 Rixen (2013); Fernandez (2015); Palan and Nesvetailova (2014); Ötsch and Schmidt (2016). Palan and Nesvetailova (2014) emphasize that the real significance of shadow banking and offshore finance is that they function as important 'black holes' in the global economy (p.31).

13 Interestingly, Frankel (2002) explains that the decomposed nature of cross-border securitization is like a set of children's Lego pieces that can be connected in different ways to produce different results (p.477).

14 In addition, US financial deregulations were designed to ease regulatory burden on securities issuance and reselling in offshore sphere since the early 1990s, making the role of OFCs as a central component of cross-border securitization (McQuiston 1991; Steinberg and Lansdale Jr 1995; Burns and McConvill 2011). First, Rule 144A establishes a nonexclusive exemption from the registration requirements of the US Securities and Exchange Commission (SEC) of 1933 for the resale of the privately placed securities by persons other than the issuer to certain qualified institutional buyers. Under the rule, Qualified Institutional Buyers (QIBs) can trade debt securities without registration and review by the SEC. Second, Regulation S provides a safe harbor from the registration requirements of the SEC of 1933 for offshore offers and sales of securities. Regulation S bond type is available for offers and trades of securities outside of the US to US and non-US QIBs. Against this background, the fraction of asset-backed securities (ABSs) under Rule144a and Regulation S had increased in OFCs since the second half of the 1990s. By the end of 2008, 34 percent of asset-backed bonds were offered privately to QIBs and about one-quarter of securities were sold in the offshore sphere (Cetorelli and Peristiani [2012], p.52).

15 In Europe, covered bonds are also important debt instruments secured by a cover pool of mortgage loans or public-sector debts, which serve as safe assets for investors in this region. They are not only a stable and cheaper source of bank funding but also important for long-term finance in Europe.

16 The main reason was that European banks turned illiquid assets into securitized products and then held large part of these on-balance sheets as eligible collateral for European Central Bank (ECB) refinancing operations (ECB 2011a, 2011c; Bakk-Simon et al. 2012).

17 Between 1999 and 2008, the issuance of ABSs in the Eurozone amounted to no more than $1,867 billion, in contrast to $11,983 billion in the US (ECB [2009], p.32).

18 Katsu (2003) is a pioneer study on the international use of the euro in terms of the development of European repo market.

19 Data from the International Capital Market Association European Repo Market Survey website.

20 See Adrian and Shin (2010), pp.1–5; Claessens et al. (2012), p.8.
21 Strange (1986/2016), p.151; Papaioannou and Portes (2008), pp.71–73; Obstfeld (2009), pp.12–13.
22 The former presidents of the ECB, Duisenberg and Trichet, stressed that the ECB will not act as role of the LLR (see Pollard [2003], p.19; Barber and Atkins 2011).
23 The Greenspan put was mainly based on the experience of deflation in Japan in the 1990s (Greenspan 2007).
24 Data from Federal Reserve Bank of St. Louis, Economic Research website.
25 There are variations to express the Greenspan put: the 'mopping-up-after strategy' (Blinder 2008) and the 'clean up after bubbles' approach (The Economist 2009).
26 The expansion of USD-denominated gross balance sheets at G-SIBs enabled them to achieve a higher return on equity (ROE) in the 2000s before the financial crisis. The level of ROEs at G-SIBs in the US and Europe was consistently at or above 20 percent, which was roughly double the ROEs in the nonfinancial sector over the period (Haldane [2010], p.13).
27 Own estimation from Acharya and Schnabl (2010), Table 4, p.55.

References

Acharya, V.V. and S. Öncü (2010), "The Repurchase Agreement (Repo Market)", in V.V. Acharya, T.F. Cooley, M.P. Richardson, and I. Walter (eds.), *Regulating Wall Street: The Dodd-Frank Act and the New Architecture of Global Finance*, Hoboken, NJ: Wiley, pp.319–350.

Acharya, V.V. and S. Öncü (2014), "A Proposal for the Resolution of Systemically Important Assets and Liabilities: The Case of the Repo Market", in V.V. Acharya, T. Beck, D.D. Evanoff, G.G. Kaufman, and R. Portes (eds.), *Social Value of the Financial Sector: Too Big to Fail or Just Too Big?* Singapore: World Scientific Publishing, pp.161–214.

Acharya V.V. and H. Schnable (2010), "Do Global Banks Spread Global Imbalances? Asset-Backed Commercial Paper during the Financial Crisis of 2007–09", *IMF Economic Review*, vol.58, issue 1, July 2010, pp.37–73.

Adrian, T. (2017), Shadow Banking and Market Based Finance, Helsinki, International Monetary Fund (IMF), September 14, 2017.

Adrian, T. and H.S. Shin (2010), "The Changing Nature of Financial Intermediation and the Financial Crisis of 2007–2009", *Federal Reserve Bank of New York Staff Reports*, no.439, March 2010.

Aglietta, M. (2000), "A Lender of Last Resort for Europe", in C.A.E. Goodhart (ed.), *Which Lender of Last Resort for Europe?* London: Central Banking Publications, pp.33–67.

Agueci, P., L. Alkan, A. Copeland, I. Davis, A. Martin, K. Pingitore, C. Prugar, T. Rivas (2014), "A Primer on the GCF Repo® Service", *Federal Reserve Bank of New York Staff Reports*, no.671, April 2014.

Altunbas, Y., L. Gambacorta, and D. Marqués (2007), "Securitisation and the Bank Lending Channel", *ECB Working Paper Series*, European Central Bank (ECB), no.383, December 2007.

Ando, M. (2012), "Recent Developments in US Dollar Funding Costs through FX Swaps", *Bank of Japan Review*, Bank of Japan (BOJ), 2012-E-3, April 2012.

Aramonte, S., A. Schrimpf, and H.S. Shin (2021/2022), "Non-Bank Financial Intermediaries and Financial Stability", *BIS Working Papers*, Bank for International Settlements (BIS), no.972, October 2021 (Revised in January 2022).

Baba, N., R.N. McCauley, and S. Ramaswamy (2009), "US Dollar Money Market Funds and Non-US banks", *BIS Quarterly Review*, Bank for International Settlements (BIS), March 2009, pp.65–80.

Bach, C.L. (2005), "US International Transactions 2004", *Survey of Current Business*, US Bureau of Economic Analysis (BEA), April 2005, pp.24–45.

Bach, C.L. (2007), "US International Transactions in 2006", *Survey of Current Business*, US Bureau of Economic Analysis (BEA), April 2007, pp.22–45.

Bakk-Simon, K., S. Borgioli, C. Giron, H. Hempell, A. Maddaloni, F. Recine, and S. Rosati (2012), "Shadow Banking System in the Euro Area: An Overview", *Occasional Paper Series*, European Central Bank (ECB), no.133, April 2012.

Baklanova, V., A. Copeland, and R. McCaughrin (2015), "Reference Guide to US Repo and Securities Lending Markets", *Federal Reserve Bank of New York Staff Report*, no.740, September 2015.

Baklanova, V., O. Dalton, and S. Tompaidis (2017), "Benefits and Risks of Central Clearing in the Repo Market", *OFR Brief Series*, Office of Financial Research (OFR), 17-04, March 9, 2017.

Barber, L. and R. Atkins (2011), "FT Interview: Jean-Claude Trichet", *Financial Times*, October 13, 2011.

Beltran, D.O., L. Pounder, and C. Thomas (2008), "Foreign Exposure to Asset-Backed Securities of US Origin", *International Finance Discussion Paper*, Board of Governors of the Federal Reserve System, no.939, August 2008.

Blinder, A.S. (2008), "Two Bubbles, Two Paths: Economic View", *New York Times*, June 15, 2008.

Brenner, R. (2002), *The Boom and the Bubble: The US in the World Economy*, London: Verso.

Bryan D., M. Rafferty, and D. Wigan (2016), "Politics, Time and Space in the Era of Shadow Banking", *Review of International Political Economy*, vol. 23, issue 6, pp.941–966.

Burns, M.J. and J. McConvill (2011), "An Unstoppable Force: The Offshore World in a Modern Global Economy", *Hastings Business Law Journal*, vol.7, issue 2, pp.205–222.

Buttonwood (2017), "The Greenspan Legacy: The Fed Chairman's Record is a Case Study in Cognitive Dissonance", *The Economist*, January 5, 2017.

Caballero, R.J. (2006), "On the Macroeconomics of Asset Shortages", *NBER Working Paper*, National Bureau of Economic Research (NBER), no.12753, December 2006.

Carbo-Valverde, S., E.J. Kane, and F. Rodriguez-Fernandez (2011), "Safety-Net Benefits Conferred on Difficult-to-Fail-and-Unwind Banks in the US and EU before and during the Great Recession", *NBER Working Paper*, National Bureau of Economic Research (NBER), no.16787, February 2011.

Cetorelli, C. and S. Peristiani (2012), "The Role of Banks in Asset Securitization", *Economic Policy Review*, vol.18, issue 2, July 2012, pp.47–63.

Chen, K., M. Fleming, J. Jackson, A. Li, and A. Sarkar (2011), "An Analysis of CDS Transactions: Implications for Public Reporting", *Federal Reserve Bank of New York Staff Reports*, no.517, September 2011.

Chesnais, F. (2016), *Finance Capital Today: Corporations and Banks in the Lasting Global Slump*, Leiden: Brill.

Claessens S., Z. Pozsar, L. Ratnovski, and M. Singh (2012), "Shadow Banking: Economics and Policy", *Staff Discussion Note*, International Monetary Fund (IMF), December 4, 2012.

Cohen, B.J. (2011), "Enlargement and the International Role of the Euro", *The Future of Global Currency: The Euro versus the Dollar*, London and New York: Routledge, pp.74–97.

Committee on the Global Financial System (CGFS) (2007), "Institutional Investors, Global Savings and Asset Allocation", *CGFS Papers*, Bank for International Settlements (BIS), no.27, February 2007.

Davies, G. (2020), "The Safe-Asset Shortage after Covid-19", *Financial Times*, June 28, 2020.

Dixon, L (2001): "Financial Flows via Offshore Financial Centres as Part of the International Financial System", *Bank of England Financial Stability Review*, Bank of England (BOE), June 2001.

Doyle, N., L. Hermans, P. Molitor, and C. Weistroffer (2016), "Shadow Banking in the Euro Area: Risks and Vulnerabilities in the Investment Fund Sector", *Occasional Paper Series*, European Central Bank (ECB), no.174, June 2016.

Eichengreen, B. (1997), The Euro as a Reserve Currency, November 1997, available at https://eml.berkeley.edu/~eichengr/research/mantokyo.pdf

Epstein, G. (2005), "Introduction" in G. Epstein (ed.), *Financialization and The World Economy*, Cheltenham and Northampton: Edward Elgar, pp.3–16.

European Central Bank (ECB) (1999), *Annual Report,* European Central Bank (ECB).

European Central Bank (ECB) (2002), "Main Features of the Repo Market in the Euro Area", *Monthly Bulletin*, European Central Bank (ECB), October 2002, pp.55–68.

European Central Bank (ECB) (2006), "The Widening of the Collateral Pool for Secured Lending in the Euro Area", *Financial Stability Review*, European Central Bank (ECB), June 2006, pp.71–73.

European Central Bank (ECB) (2007), TARGET 2 Securities Blueprint, European Central Bank (ECB), March 8, 2007.

European Central Bank (ECB) (2009), "The International Role of the Euro in the Market for Asset-Backed Securities", *The International Role of the Euro*, European Central Bank (ECB), July 2009, pp.31–34.

European Central Bank (ECB) (2011a), Recent Developments Securitisation, European Central Bank (ECB), February 2011.

European Central Bank (ECB) (2011b), *The International Role of the Euro*, European Central Bank (ECB), July 2011.

European Central Bank (ECB) (2011c), "The Supply of Money-Bank Behaviour and the Implications for Monetary Analysis", *Monthly Bulletin*, European Central Bank (ECB), October 2011, pp.63–79.

European Central Bank (ECB) (2012), *Financial Integration in Europe*, European Central Bank (ECB), April 2012.

European Central Bank (ECB) (2014), *Euro Repo Market: Improvement for Collateral and Liquidity Management*, European Central Bank (ECB), July 2014.

Ewehart, C. and J. Tapking (2008), "Repo Markets, Counterparty Risk and the 2007/2008 Liquidity Crisis", *ECB Working Paper Series*, European Central Bank (ECB), no.909, June 2008.

Federal Deposit Insurance Corporation (FDIC) (2006), "A New Plateau for the US Securitization Market", *FDIC Outlook*, Federal Deposit Insurance Corporation (FDIC), Fall 2006, pp.3–10.

Fernandez, R. (2015), "Shadow Banking and European Offshore Financial Centres: The Blind Spot in EU Policy Debates", *FEPS Policy Brief*, Foundation for European Progressive Studies (FEPS), April 2015.

Fichtner, J. (2016), "The Anatomy of the Cayman Islands Offshore Financial Center: Anglo-America, Japan, and the Role of Hedge Funds", *Review of International Political Economy*, vol.23, issue 6, pp.1034–1063.

Financial Stability Board (FSB) (2015), *Transforming Shadow Banking into Resilient Market-Based Finance: An Overview of Progress*, Financial Stability Board (FSB), November 12, 2015.

Financial Stability Board (FSB) (2019), *Global Shadow Banking Monitoring Report 2018*, Financial Stability Board (FSB), February 4, 2019.

Fleming, M.J. (2000), "The Benchmark US Treasury Market: Recent Performance and Possible Alternatives", *FRBNY Economic Policy Review*, Federal Reserve Bank of New York, April 2000.

Folkerts-Landau, D. and P.M. Garber. (1992), "The European Central Bank or a Monetary Policy Rule", *NBER Working Papers Series*, National Bureau of Economic Research (NBER), no.4016, March 1992.

Foster, J.B. and F. Magdoff (2009), *The Great Financial Crisis: Causes and Consequences*, New York: Monthly Review Press.

Frankel, T. (1998), "Cross-Border Securitization: Without Law, But Not Lawless", *Duke Journal of Comparative & International Law*, vol.8, issue 2, Spring 1998, pp.255–282.

Frankel, T. (2002), "The Law of Cross-Border Securitization: Lex Juris", *Duke Journal of Comparative and International Law*, vol.12, issue 2, Spring 2002, pp.475–492.

Gabor, D. (2016a), "A Step Too Far: The European Financial Transactions Tax on Shadow Banking", *Journal of European Public Policy*, vol.23, issue 6, pp.925–945.

Gabor, D. (2016b), "The (Impossible) Repo Trinity: The Political Economy of Repo Markets", *Review of International Political Economy*, vol.23, issue 6, pp.967–1000.

Gabor, D. and C. Ban (2015), "Banking on Bonds: The New Links between States and Markets", *Journal of Common Market Studies*, vol.54, issue 3, pp.617–635.

Garbade, K.D. (2006), "The Evolution of Repo Contracting Conventions in the 1980s", *FRBNY Economic Policy Review*, Federal Reserve Bank of New York, May 2006, pp.27–42.

Gerdesmeier, D., F.P. Mongelli, and B. Roffia (2007), "The Eurosystem, the US Federal Reserve and the Bank of Japan: Similarities and Differences", *Working Paper Series*, European Central Bank (ECB), no.742, March 2007.

Gorton, G. and T. Muir (2015), *Mobile Collateral versus Immobile Collateral*, BIS Annual Conference in Lucerne, Switzerland, Bank for International Settlements (BIS), April 27, 2015.

Green, J. (2016), "Anglo-American Development, the Euromarkets, and the Deeper Origins of Neoliberal Deregulation", *Review of International Studies*, vol.42, issue 3, pp.425–449.

Greenspan, A. (2002), *Remarks by Chairman Alan Greenspan, Before the Economic Club of New York, New York City*, Board of Governors of the Federal Reserve System, December 19, 2002.

Greenspan, A. (2007), *The Age of Turbulence: Adventures in a New World*, New York: Penguin Press.

Hakkarainen, P. (2014), *Shadow Banking-What Kind of Regulation for the (European) Shadow Banking System?* Central Bank Speech, Bank for International Settlements (BIS), November 14, 2014.

Haldane, A. (2010), "The Contribution of the Financial Sector: Miracle or Mirage?", Paper Presented at the Future of Finance Conference, London, Bank of England (BOE), July 14, 2010.

Hampton, M. and J. Abbott (eds.) (1999), *Offshore Finance Centers and Tax Havens: The Rise of Global Capital*, London: Palgrave Macmillan.

Harvey, D. (2010), *The Enigma of Capital: And the Crises of Capitalism*, New York: Oxford University Press.

He, D. and R. McCauley (2012), "Eurodollar Banking and Currency Internationalisation", *BIS Quarterly Review*, Bank for International Settlements (BIS), June 2012, pp.33–46.

Herr, H. (2014), "The European Central Bank and the US Federal Reserve as Lender of Last Resort", *Panoeconomicus*, vol.1, pp.59–78.

Hodula, M. (2018), "Off the Radar: Exploring the Rise of Shadow Banking in the EU", *Czech National Bank Working Paper*, Czech National Bank (CNB), no.16/2018, December 2018.

Hördahl, P. and M.R. King (2008), "Developments in Repo Markets during the Financial Turmoil", *BIS Quarterly Review*, Bank for International Settlements (BIS), December 2008, pp.37–53.

Hossein-Zadeh, I. (2014), *Beyond Mainstream Explanations of the Financial Crisis: Parasitic Finance Capital*, New York: Routledge.

International Capital Market Association (ICMA) (2014), "Collateral is the New Cash: The Systemic Risks of Inhibiting Collateral Fluidity", International Capital Market Association (ICMA), April 2014.

International Monetary Fund (IMF) (2014), "How Big Is the Implicit Subsidy for Banks Considered Too Important to Fail?" *Global Financial Stability Report*, International Monetary Fund (IMF), April 2014, pp.101–132.

Isaac, D. and F.C. Reed, Jr (2017), "Government-Sponsored Enterprises and Federal Agencies", in G. Strumeyer and S. Swammy (eds.), *The Capital Markets: Evolution of the Financial Ecosystem*, Hoboken, NJ: Willey, pp.210–231.

Johnson, S. and J. Kwak (2010), *13 Bankers: The Wall Street Takeover and Next Financial Meltdown*, New York: Pantheon Books.

Katsu, E. (2003), "European Repo Market: From Viewpoint of International Use of the Euro", *Shouken Keizai Kenkyu*, Japan Securities Research Institute (JSRI), no.42, June 2003, pp.139–153 (in Japanese).

Kozak, S. and O. Teplova (2012), "Securitization as a Tool of Bank Liquidity and Funding Management before and after the Crisis: The Case of the EU", *Financial Internet Quarterly: e-Finanse*, vol.8, issue 4, pp.30–43.

Maes, S. (2015), "Shadow Banking: A European Perspective", in S. Claessens, D. Evanoff, G. Kaufman, and L. Laeven (eds.), *Shadow Banking within and across National Borders*, Singapore: World Scientific Publishing, pp.347–372.

Mallaby, S. (2016), *The Man Who Knew: The Life and Times of Alan Greenspan*, New York: Penguin Press.

McCauley, R.N. (2012), "The Euro and the Yen as Anchor Currencies: Before and during the Financial Crisis-Comments on Moss's Paper "The Euro: Internationalised at Birth" and Takagi's Paper "Internationalising the Yen, 1984–2003: Unfinished Agenda or Mission Impossible?"" *BIS Papers*, Bank for International Settlements (BIS), no.61, January 2012, pp.93–104.

McGuire, P. (2004), "A Shift in London's Eurodollar Market", *BIS Quarterly Review*, Bank for International Settlements (BIS), September 2004, pp.67–78.

McGuire, P. and N. Tarashev (2007), "International Banking with the Euro", *BIS Quarterly Review*, Bank for International Settlements (BIS), December 2007, pp.47–61.

McNally, D. (2011), *Global Slump: The Economics and Politics of Crisis and Resistance*, Oakland, CA: PM Press.

McQuiston, R.W. (1991), "Rule 144A, Regulation S and Amending Glass-Steagall Act: A New Look at Foreign Banks and Foreign Issuers Participating in the United States Securities Market", *Syracuse Journal of International Law and Commerce*, no.171, pp.171–239.

Menand, L. (2022), *The Fed Unbound: Central Banking in a Time of Crisis*, New York: Columbia Global Reports.

Metrick, A. and D. Tarullo (2021), Congruent Financial Regulation, *Brookings Papers on Economic Activity*, Spring 2021, pp.143–181.

Moutot, P., A. Jung, and F.P. Mongelli (2008), "The Workings of the Eurosystem: Monetary Policy Preparations and Decision-Making", *ECB Occasional Paper Series*, European Central Bank (ECB), no.79, January 2008.

Norfield, T. (2016), *The City: London and the Global Power of Finance*, London: Verso.

Obstfeld, M. (2009), "Lenders of Last Resort in a Globalized World", Coleman Fung Risk Management Research Center, Institute of Business and Economic Research, UC Berkeley, January 2009.

O'Driscoll, G.P. Jr. (2009), "Money and the Present Crisis", *Cato Journal*, vol.29, issue 1, pp.167–186.

Office of Financial Research (OFR) (2024), *Annual Reports 2024,* Office of Financial Research (OFR).

Ötsch, S. and M. Schmidt (2016), "Offshore Financial Centres and Tax Evasion in Banking", in I. Ertürk and D. Gabor (eds.), *The Routledge Companion to Banking Regulation and Reform*, Abingdon: Routledge, pp.272–292.

Palan, R. (2003), *The Offshore World: Sovereign Markets, Virtual Places, and Nomad Millionaires*, Ithaca, NY: Cornell University Press.

Palan, R., R. Murphy, and C. Chavagneux (2010), *Tax Heavens: How Globalization Really Works,* Ithaca, NY: Cornell University Press.

Palan, R. and A. Nesvetailova (2014), "Elsewhere, Ideally Nowhere: Shadow Banking and Offshore Finance", *Politik*, vol.6, issue 4, pp.26–34.

Palley, T.I. (2012), *From Financial Crisis to Stagnation: The Destruction of Shared Prosperity and the Role of Economics*, New York: Cambridge University Press.

Panitch, L. and S. Gindin (2012), *The Making of Global Capitalism: The Political Economy of American Empire*, London: Verso.

Papadoa-Schioppa, T. (2000), "EMU and Banking Supervision", in C.A.E. Goodhart (ed.), *Which Lender of Last Resort for Europe?* London: Central Banking Publications, pp.13–29.

Papaioannou, E. and R. Portes (2008), "Costs and Benefits of Running an International Currency", *Economic Papers*, European Commission, no.348, November 2008.

Patalano, R. and C. Roulet (2020), "Structural Developments in Global Financial Intermediation: The Rise of Debt and Non-Bank Credit Intermediation", *OECD Working Papers on Finance, Insurance and Private Pensions*, Organisation for Economic Co-operation and Development (OECD), no.44.

Pollard, S.P. (2003), "A Look Inside Two Central Banks: The European Central Bank and the Federal Reserve", *Review*, Federal Reserve Bank of St. Louis, January/February 2003, pp.11–30.

Pozsar, Z. (2011), "Institutional Cash Pools and the Triffin Dilemma of the US Banking System", *IMF Working Paper*, International Monetary Fund (IMF), 11/190, August 2011.

Pozsar, Z. (2014), "Shadow Banking: The Money View", *Working Paper*, Office of Financial Research (OFR), 14-04, July 2, 2014.

Pozsar, Z. (2015), *A Macro View of Shadow Banking. Levered Betas and Wholesale Funding in the Context of Secular Stagnation*, January 31, 2015, available at SSRN: https://ssrn.com/abstract=2558945 or https://dx. doi.org/10.2139/ssrn.2558945

Pozsar Z. and M. Singh (2011), "The Nonbank-Bank Nexus and the Shadow Banking System", *IMF Working Paper*, International Monetary Fund (IMF), 11/289, December 2011.

Pozsar, Z., A. Tobias, A. Ashcraft, and H. Boesky (2010/2012), "Shadow Banking", *Federal Reserve Bank of New York Staff Report*, no.458, July 2010 (Revised in February 2012).

Prati, A. and G.J. Schinasi (1997), "EMU and International Capital Markets: Structural Implications and Risks", in P.R. Masson, T.H. Krueger, and B.G. Turtelboom (eds.), *EMU and the International Monetary System*, Washington DC: International Monetary Fund (IMF), pp.263–388.

Rixen, T. (2013), "Why Reregulation after the Crisis Is Feeble: Shadow Banking, Offshore Financial Centers, and Jurisdictional Competition", *Regulation & Governance*, vol.7, issue 4, pp.435–459.

Schinasi, G.J., C.F. Kramer, and R.T. Smith (2001), "Financial Implications of the Shrinking Supply of US Treasury Securities", *IMF Working Paper*, International Monetary Fund (IMF), 01/61, May 2001.

Schinasi, G.J. and P.G. Teixeira (2006), "The Lender of Last Resort in the European Single Financial Market", *IMF Working Paper*, International Monetary Fund (IMF), 06/127, May 2006.

Schwarcz, S.L. (2002), "The Universal Language of International Securitization", *Duke Journal of Comparative & International Law*, vol.12, issue 2, January 2002, pp.285–308.

Sharman, L.C. (2006), *Havens in a Storm: The Struggle for Global Tax Regulation*, Ithaca, NY: Cornell University Press.

Shaxson, N. (2011), *Treasure Islands: Tax Havens and the Men Who Stole the World*, New York: St. Martin's Press.

Shaxson, N. (2019), *The Finance Curse: How Global Finance Is Making Us All Poorer*, New York: Grove Press.

Shin, H.S. (2012), "Global Banking Glut and Loan Risk Premium", *IMF Economic Review*, International Monetary Fund (IMF), vol.60, issue 2, pp.155–192.

Steinberg, M.I. and D.L. Lansdale Jr (1995), "Regulation S and Rule 144A: Creating a Workable Fiction in an Expanding Global Securities Market", *International Lawyer*, vol.29, issue 1, Spring 1995, pp.43–64.

Strange, S. (1986/2016), *Casino Capitalism*, Manchester: Manchester University Press.

Talani, L.S. (2012), *Globalization, Hegemony and the Future of the City of London*, New York: Palgrave Macmillan.

The Economist (2009), The Roots of the "Clean Up after Bubbles" Approach, *The Economist*, August 21, 2009.

The Financial Crisis Inquiry Commission (2011), *The Financial Crisis Inquiry Report: Final Report of the National Commission on the Causes of the Financial and Economic Crisis in the United States*, Washington DC: US Government Printing Office, January 2011.

The Giovannini Group (1999), EU Repo Markets: Opportunities for Change, European Commission, October 1999.

Tokunaga, J. (2019), "The Comparative Advantage of the US Shadow Banking System and the Role of the US Dollar", *The Japanese Political Economy*, vol.45, issue 1–2, May 2019, pp.20–42.

Tokunaga, J. and G. Epstein (2018), "The Endogenous Finance of Global-Dollar-Based Financial Fragility in the 2000s: A Minskyan Approach", *Review of Keynesian Economics*, vol.6, issue 1, January 2018, pp.62–82.

Urry, J. (2014), *Offshoring*, Cambridge and Malden, MA: Polity.

Wójcik, D. (2013), "The Dark Side of NY-LON: Financial Centres and the Global Financial Crisis", *Urban Studies*, vol.50, issue 13, pp.2736–2752.

Part III

The nature of the US dollar standard system

4 The endogenous finance of the global dollar in the shadow banking system in the 2000s

1 Dealer banks in the shadow banking system

As analyzed in Chapter 3, the comparative advantage of the US shadow banking system over the one in the Eurozone could encouraged global systemically important banks (G-SIBs) to denominate their gross balance sheets in the dollar, rather than the euro, in the 2000s in the run-up to Global Financial Crisis (GFC) of 2007–09. The deeper question is how G-SIBs could draw short-term dollar borrowing that enabled them to expand their gross balance sheets denominated in the dollar in the 2000s. To respond to the question, it is important to closely discuss how dealer banks, central subsidiaries of G-SIBs, play critical roles in interfacing with many different entities in the shadow banking system. Starting with a bird's-eye perspective on financial intermediation in the shadow banking system as seen in Figure 3.3, dealer banks, also known as investment banks, play a central role in collateral intermediation, in which dealers act as middlemen between the long pools and the cash pools by transferring simultaneously cash and collateral assets. To do so, dealer banks are generally involved in gross balance sheets positions called 'matched book' intermediation between repos and reverse repos. Figure 4.1 is a stylized T-account of the matched book intermediation, which helps us to understand how dealer banks create endogenously repo liabilities using US Treasury securities as collateral assets, which helped G-SIBs borrow short-term dollar funds.

On the one hand, hedge funds borrow cash by delivering US Treasury securities as collateral assets through the reverse repos on bilateral repo markets, and dealer banks lend the cash to them. The hedge funds, in turn, buy the MBS with the cash. On the other hand, the dealer bank can fund its lending by borrowing cash from the cash pool including money market mutual funds (MMMFs) through repos on tri-party repo markets, using the US Treasury securities as collateral assets. With respect to the latter, the dealer bank accommodates credit demand for safe, short-term liquid instruments (i.e., repo liabilities) denominated in the dollar from the cash pool. In other words, the dealer banks issue endogenously dollar funds through repos.[1]

DOI: 10.4324/9781003733959-7

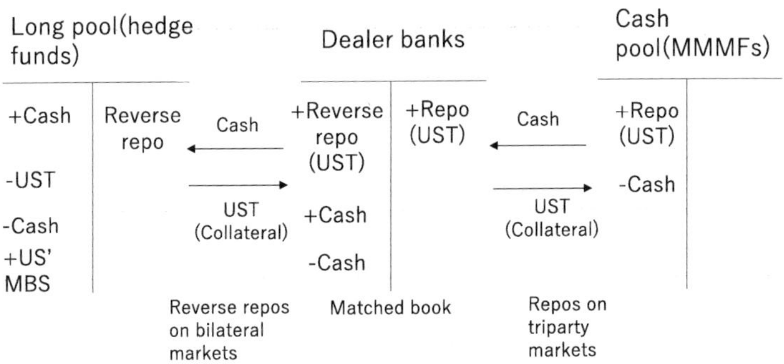

Figure 4.1 A Stylized T-Account of the Matched Book Intermediation at Dealer Banks

Sources: Own elaboration on Stigum (1989), p.285; Stigum and Crescenzi (2007), p.562; Mehrling et al. (2013), p.3; Pozsar (2013, 2014, 2015); Gabor and Vestergaard (2016), pp.19–21; CGFS (2017), pp.5–6; Carlson and Macchiavelli (2018); Sissoko (2019), p.8; Wullweber (2020), p.10; Özgür (2021), p.9; Afonso et al. (2021), pp.4–7.

Note: UST = US Treasury securities; MMMFs = money market mutual funds.

2 Global repurchase agreements

Repos are heavily traded in global financial system (Di Luigi, Perrella and Ruggieri 2024), in which dealer banks create endogenously global dollar funds.[2] Today, the international repo market is huge, representing $8–10 trillion of collateral assets (Howell [2020], p.91). For instance, US dealer banks created endogenously cross-border repo liabilities vis-à-vis nonbank financial institutions (NBFIs)' clients, including mutual funds and hedge funds in offshore financial centers (OFCs) such as the UK and the Caribbean financial centers in the 2000s before the GFC. This can be seen in the following quotations from the Survey of Current Business by the US Bureau of Economic Analysis (BEA) in the 2000s prior to the GFC:

> Liabilities of US securities brokers (dealer banks: author) increased $172.1 billion in 2004, following an increase of $165.3 billion in 2003. Sizable borrowing by US brokers from foreign nonbanks reflected an increase in repurchase activity, in large part with international mutual funds and hedge funds in the Caribbean.
>
> (Bach (2005), p.43)

> Liabilities of US securities brokers increased $32.7 billion in 2006, compared with an increase of $13.0 billion in 2005. The increase was largely in the form of repurchase agreements with nonbanks in the United Kingdom.
>
> (Bach [2007], p.42)

> Liabilities reported by US banks and securities brokers increased $510.9 billion in 2007, up from an increase of $434.4 billion in 2006…Much of the increase resulted from borrowing in the first half of the year (2007: author) when US securities brokers borrowed heavily through repurchase agreements.
>
> (Bach [2008], p.44)

In addition to the creation of cross-border repo liabilities vis-à-vis NBFIs' clients in OFCs, global dealer banks rapidly expanded their gross internal repo borrowing vis-à-vis their own foreign subsidiaries in the run-up to the GFC. Figure 4.2 provides a stylized illustration of the various segments of the internal capital market within a US bank holding company.

With respect to segment (3), US dealer banks expanded their gross internal repos and securities lending vis-à-vis their own foreign subsidiaries. More specifically, US primary dealers took collateral assets posted by their US clients and financed it at the globally cheapest markets like the UK without leverage limit in the pre-GFC period (Gupta [2021], p.10). As a result, internal liabilities of US primary dealers nearly quadrupled over the pre-GFC period to $1.2 trillion in the quarter of 2007 (Gupta [2021], p.12).

Against this backdrop, outstanding cross-border repos liabilities issued by US financial institutions increased abruptly from $151 billion in 2001, when its data became available, to about $1 trillion in 2006.[3] Thus, the issuance of cross-border repos by dealer banks became one of the largest components in the endogenous finance of short-term dollar liabilities across the US border and outside the US (i.e., global dollar supply) in the 2000s before the GFC.

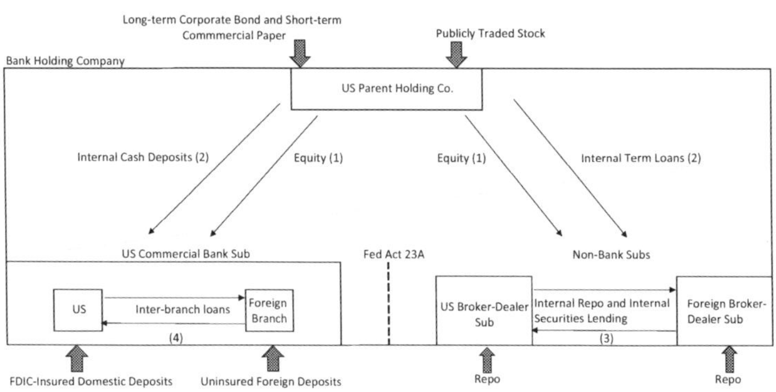

Figure 4.2 Stylized Diagram of Internal Capital Markets in US Banking Holding Company

Source: Reproduced and revised from Gupta (2021), Figure 1, p.9.

Note: FDIC = Federal Deposit Insurance Corporation.

In retrospect, it has been acknowledged that commercial banks in a few international currency countries create short-term liabilities for nonresidents, called often foreign balances, which perform as international currency for settling various financial obligations and transactions involving foreign exchange transactions. In the case of international settlements denominated in US dollar involving foreign exchange transactions, dollar balances issued by US commercial banks serve as international money, underpinned through Fedwire and privately large-value payments platforms including Clearing House Interbank Payment System (CHIPS) and major messaging networks such as the Society for Worldwide Interbank Financial Telecommunication (SWIFT).[4]

Compared to the volume of studies covering dollar balances created by US commercial banks, academic literature is relatively young in its exploration of how dealer banks, central subsidiaries of G-SIBs, endogenously create the global dollar in the shadow banking system.[5]

To begin with, we understand how dealer banks are involved in trading, clearing, and settlement through repos in a closed and domestic economy. Consider now trading, clearing, and settlement in general collateral finance (GCF) repos, which are a popular service for dealer banks in US repo markets. Figure 4.3 is a stylized example of the GCF repo between dealer bank A and dealer bank B.

In the first step (trading), dealer bank A and dealer bank B negotiate, anonymously, through an interbank dealer (IDB). In the second step (clearance), the IDB then sends settlement instructions to the Fixed Income Clearing Corporation (FICC) as a central counterparty (CCP) which becomes the legal counterparty to both dealer bank A and dealer bank B. In the third step (settlement), the FICC provides netting services in the process, and net position of cash and securities as collateral assets is settled via a clearing bank. At the end of each trading day, the FICC computes the amounts of cash and securities

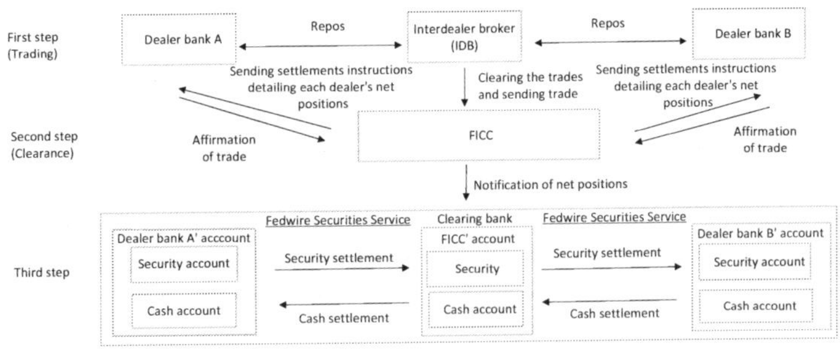

Figure 4.3 A Stylized Example of GCF Repo Trading, Clearance, and Settlement

Sources: Translated and reproduced from Nakajima and Shukuwa (2008), Figure 5–14, p.148. Part of this figure is revised on Agueci et al. (2014), pp.12–15.

that dealer bank A promised to deliver and the amount that was promised to another dealer bank B. The difference between these two amounts (i.e., each position of the dealer banks) is settled through the Fedwire Securities Service, which is a real-time delivery versus payment (DVP) securities settlement system at the US Fed. Direct participation is restricted to depository institutions, typically commercial banks under the Fedwire Securities Service; dealer banks cannot debit or credit a reserve account at the Fed. Instead, dealer banks have come to rely on commercial banks to act as their clearing banks to settle the DVP-securities settlement on the Fedwire Securities Service (SIFMA 1999). Similar to the tri-party repo market, two clearing banks, Bank of New York Mellon and JP Morgan Chase, settled the GCF repo transactions. Because JP Morgan Chase closed its tri-party business by the end of 2017, Bank of New York Mellon is the only provider of this service. The clearing bank receives instructions from the FICC to settle each dealer bank's net positions, and then settles the net position not only by transferring securities from the dealer bank A's security account to the dealer bank B's security account, but also by simultaneously transferring cash from the dealer bank B's cash account to the dealer bank A's cash account. As such, dealer banks serve as intermediating given cash, which are held as deposit balances created by their clearing banks, in exchange for pledged securities as collateral assets. In this regard, dealer banks appear to play a passive role of financial intermediaries in US repo markets.

Extending the stylized interpretation of the passive role of financial intermediation by dealer banks in US repo markets into a global context would suggest that the creation of cross-border repo's liabilities by dealers may be characterized as their passively international financial intermediary, because they transfer the ownership of existing dollar balances across the borders in exchange for securities as collateral on a global scale.

3 The endogenously elastic finance of the global dollar in the shadow banking system

However, the stylized interpretation regarding the role of dealer banks as passively international financial intermediation lacks understanding how dynamic global dealers function as an engine for mining and intermediating collateral assets on a global scale, i.e., global collateral plumbing.[6] Dealer banks pursue the global financial plumbing of the collateral assets in the international bilateral collateral market. The size of the global bilateral collateral market, where the global money and collateral exchange take place, was US$10 trillion in 2007 (Singh [2017], p.10).[7] Only a small number of large banks and dealer banks (e.g., 10–15 large banks) play a central role in the global financial plumbing, with many different types of entities within G-SIBs and outside them, as can be seen in the following important quotations from Singh and Goel (2019):

> The financial system that includes banks, hedge funds, pension funds, insurers, sovereign wealth funds (SWFs), etc. be represented by entities A to Z. Only a small number (say XYZ) have the capabilities to regularly move financial collateral across borders on a large scale. XYZ also happen to be the large 10–15 banks. Major dealers active in the collateral industry include Goldman Sachs, Morgan Stanley, JP Morgan, Bank of America/Merrill, and Citibank in the US. In Europe and elsewhere, important collateral dealers are Deutsche Bank, UBS, Barclays, Credit Suisse, Société Générale, BNP Paribas, HSBC, Royal Bank of Scotland (with a declining share), and Nomura. Recently Canadian banks have also entered this market.
>
> (p.8; underline is by author)

> The remaining financial entities, from A to Z, that demand and supply collateral need to connect with each other via XYZ. Entry into this market is not prohibited but is extremely expensive and difficult, as it requires having a global footprint and global clients…For example, a Chilean pension fund may want Indonesian bonds for six months, and W (for example, a hedge fund, or a securities lender in Hong Kong) may be holding these bonds and is willing to rent out to A for six months for a small fee. But W does not know there is demand from A. Only via XYZ can A connect to W. Since XYZ sits in the middle of the web, they have the ability to optimize in ways that give them an advantage. The Indonesian bonds may come into their possession because XYZ loaned W money, or because XYZ have a derivative with W, or through a security lending agreement. Such securities that need to move cross-borders under a "repo," or "security lending," or related transaction need to be legally perfected…
>
> (p.8; underlines are by author)

In addition, the optimization of global collateral plumbing allows dealer banks to reuse collateral assets (i.e., rehypothecation) provided by clients. Specifically, a client provides a security as collateral asset in exchange for cash and grants the dealers the right to repledge this collateral. The dealers can then reuse this security as collateral to another client to source the cash through repo on the US tri-party market (Kirk et al. [2014], pp.132–134). Thus, the flexibilities of the rehypothecation allow dealer banks to generate elastically internal dollar financing without the need to attract additional funding from the external financial markets (Kirk et al. [2014], pp.134–136). Thus, the development of global collateral plumbing, one of the most remarkable financial innovations and evolutions in the shadow banking system, enabled global dealers to endogenously create more elastic and leveraged short-term global dollar liabilities, although the global dollar liabilities created endogenously in this way in the shadow banking system is not ex nihilo as traditional and commercial banks' credit creation.[8]

Therefore, it can be presumed that the dynamics in global collateral plumbing enabled dealer banks to endogenously create the global dollar in the shadow banking system, which was more elastic and leveraged than that of the traditional banking system in the 2000s.

Notes

1 Aglietta (1985) was a pioneering study that analyzed the endogenous supply of the global dollar in the Eurodollar market since the 1970s, which had increasingly been dissociated from the dollar supply by the US balance of payments deficit.

2 CGFS (2020) illustrates an example of global dollar funding where non-US repo dealer banks play a central role for intermediating dollar funds on a global scale (p.34).

3 Data from the Board of Governors of Federal Reserve System website.

4 Faudot (2018).

5 Since the GFC of 2007–09, it has been debated among heterodox scholars on whether short-term liquid liabilities, which are called often shadow money, created by NBFIs such as dealer banks, can be regarded as new type of money or not (Gabor and Vestergaard 2016, 2018; Nersisyan and Dantas 2017; Sgambati 2018). Most of heterodox scholar stresses that short-term liquid liabilities issued by NBFIs such as dealer banks do not serve as final means of payment and settlement, contrary to bank deposits created by commercial banks that perform as major means of payments and settlements of various financial obligations and transactions (Michell 2017, p.361; Bouguelli 2020; Tropeano 2018, pp.80–82; Caverzasi, Botta and Capelli 2019, p.1045).

6 Murau (2017) refers to the collateral exchange in repos as merely a by-product of credit creation (p.809). But it is apparent that collateral flow is not simply the opposite of funding but has its own special characteristics (Aguiar et al. 2016).

7 Moreover, global collateral plumbing by G-SIBs is, in part, intermediated through OFCs. Given the premier position of London as a global hub for collateral and liquidity management (Lysandrou, Nesvetailova and Palan 2017, pp.176–177), London can be considered a central node of global collateral plumbing.

8 Howell (2020) and Wullweber (2020) emphasize that the shadow banking makes credit creation more elastic than the traditional banking without creating much new lending.

References

Afonso, G., M. Cipriani, A. Copeland, A. Kovner, G.L. Spada, and A. Martin (2021), "The Market Events of Mid-September 2019", Economic Policy Review, vol.27, issue 2, pp.1–24.

Aglietta, M. (1985), "The Creation of International Liquidity", in L. Tsoukalis (ed.), *The Political Economy of International Money: In Search of a New Order*, London: Royal Institute of International Affairs; London; Beverly Hills: Sage Publications, pp.171–202.

Agueci, P., L. Alkan, A. Copeland, I. Davis, A. Martin, K. Pingitore, C. Prugar, and T. Rivas (2014), "A Primer on the GCF Repo® Service", *Federal Reserve Bank of New York Staff Reports*, no.671, April 2014.

Aguiar, A., R. Bookstaber, D.Y. Kenett, and T. Wipf (2016), "A Map of Collateral Uses and Flows", *OFR Working Paper Series*, Office of Financial Research (OFR), 16-6, May 26, 2016.

Bach, C.L. (2005), "US International Transactions 2004", *Survey of Current Business*, US Bureau of Economic Analysis (BEA), April 2005, pp.24–45.

Bach, C.L. (2007), "US International Transactions in 2006", *Survey of Current Business*, US Bureau of Economic Analysis (BEA), April 2007, pp.22–45.

Bach, C.L. (2008), "US International Transactions in 2007", *Survey of Current Business*, US Bureau of Economic Analysis (BEA), April 2008, pp.22–47.

Bouguelli, R. (2020), "Is Shadow Banking Really Akin to Banking? A Critical Analysis in Light of Monetary Theory", *Journal of Post Keynesian Economics*, vol.43, issue 1, pp.1–27.

Carlson, M. and M. Macchiavelli (2018), "Emergency Collateral Upgrade", *Finance and Economics Discussion Series*, Board of Governors of the Federal Reserve System, 2018-078, November 2018.

Caverzasi, E., A. Botta, and C. Capelli (2019), "Shadow Banking and the Financial Side of Financialisation", *Cambridge Journal of Economics*, vol.43, issue 4, pp.1029–1051.

Committee on the Global Financial System (CGFS) (2017), "Repo Market Functioning", *CGFS Papers*, Bank for International Settlements (BIS), no.59, April 2017.

Committee on the Global Financial System (CGFS) (2020), "US Dollar Funding: An International Perspective", *CGFS Papers*, Bank for International Settlements (BIS), no.65, June 2020.

Di Luigi, C., A. Perrella, and A. Ruggieri (2024), "The Fundamental Role of the Repo Market and Central Clearing", *Markets, Infrastructures, Payment Systems Series*, Bank of Italy, no.48, July 2024.

Faudot, A. (2018), "The US Dollar and Its Payments System: Architecture and Political Implications", *Review of Keynesian Economics*, vol.6, issue 1, pp.83–95.

Gabor, D. and J. Vestergaard (2016), Toward a Theory of Shadow Money, *INET Working Paper*, Institute for New Economic Thinking (INET), April 2016.

Gabor, G. and J. Vestergaard (2018), "Chasing Unicorns: The European Single Safe Asset Project", *Competition & Change*, vol.22, issue 2, pp.139–164.

Gupta, A. (2021), "The Internal Capital Markets of Global Dealer Banks", *Finance and Economics Discussion Series*, Board of Governors of the Federal Reserve System, 2021-036, June 7, 2021.

Howell, M.J. (2020), *Capital Wars: The Rise of Global Liquidity*, Basingstoke: Palgrave Macmillan.

Kirk, A., J. McAndrews, P. Sastry, and P. Weed (2014), "Matching Collateral Supply and Financing Demands in Dealer Banks", *FRBNY Economic Policy Review*, Federal Reserve Bank of New York, December 2014, pp.127–151.

Lysandrou, P., A. Nesvetailova, and R. Palan, (2017), "The Best of Both Worlds: Scale Economies and Discriminatory Policies in London's Global Financial Centre", *Economy and Society*, vol.46, issue 2, pp.159–184.

Mehrling, P., Z. Pozsar, J. Sweeney, and D.H. Nielson (2013), *Bagehot Was a Shadow Banker: Shadow Banking*, Central Banking, and the Future of Global Finance, November 5, 2013.

Michell, J. (2017), "Do Shadow Banks Create Money? 'Financialisation' and the Monetary Circuit", *Metroeconomica*, vol.68, issue 2, pp.354–377.

Murau, S. (2017), "Shadow Money and the Public Money Supply: The Impact of the 2007–2009 Financial Crisis on the Monetary System", *Review of International Political Economy*, vol.24, issue 5, pp.802–838.

Nakajima, M. and S. Shukuwa (2008), *Securities Settlement System*, Second Edition, Tokyo: Toyo Keizai Sinposha (in Japanese).

Nersisyan, Y. and F. Dantas (2017), "Rethinking Liquidity Creation: Banks, Shadow Banks and the Elasticity of Finance", *Journal of Post Keynesian Economics*, vol.40, issue 3, pp.279–299.

Özgür, G. (2021), "Shadow Banking and Financial Intermediation", *Metroeconomica*, vol.72 issue 4, November 2021, pp.731–757.

Pozsar, Z. (2013), *The Global Financial Ecosystem, VoxEU*, Center for Economic Policy Research (CEPR), November 7, 2013.

Pozsar, Z. (2014), "Shadow Banking: The Money View", *Working Paper*, Office of Financial Research (OFR), 14-04, July 2, 2014.

Pozsar, Z. (2015), *A Macro View of Shadow Banking. Levered Betas and Wholesale Funding in the Context of Secular Stagnation*, January 31, 2015, available at SSRN: https://ssrn.com/abstract=2558945 or https://dx.doi.org/10.2139/ssrn.2558945

Securities Industry and Financial Markets Association (SIFMA) (1999), "4. Clearance and Settlement Infrastructure", Uniform Practices for the Clearance and Settlement of Mortgage-Backed Securities and Other Related Securities, Securities Industry and Financial Markets Association (SIFMA).

Sgambati, S. (2018), "The Art of Leverage: A Study of Bank Power, Money-Making and Debt Finance", *Review of International Political Economy*, vol.26, issue 2, pp.287–312.

Singh, M. (2017), "Collateral Reuse and Balance Sheet Space", *IMF Working Paper*, International Monetary Fund (IMF), 17/113, April 2017.

Singh, M. and R. Goel (2019), "Pledged Collateral Market's Role in Transmission to Short-Term Market Rates", *IMF Working Paper*, International Monetary Fund (IMF), 19/106, May 2019.

Sissoko, C. (2019), "Repurchase Agreements and the (De)construction of Financial Markets", *Economy & Society*, vol. 48, issue 3, pp.315–341.

Stigum, M. (1989), *The Repo and Reverse Markets*, Homewood, IL: Dow Jones-Irwin.

Stigum, M. and A. Crescenzi (2007), *Stigum's Money Market*, Fourth Edition, New York: McGraw-Hill.

Tropeano, D. (2018), *Financial Regulation in the European Union after the Crisis: A Minskian Approach*, London: Routledge.

Wullweber, J. (2020), "The Politics of Shadow Money: Security Structures, Money Creation and Unconventional Central Banking", *New Political Economy*, vol.26, issue 1, pp.69–85.

5 Global financial fragility during the US housing bubble and the Global Financial Crisis of 2007–09

1 The changes in financial conditions during the US housing bubble

As demonstrated in Figure 1.2, gross capital flows expanded rapidly from 24.4 percent in 2004 to 43.3 percent in 2007 in the run-up to the Global Financial Crisis (GFC). The rapid expansion of gross capital flows reflected, in part, the dynamically overstretched nature of gross balance sheets denominated in the dollar at global systemically important banks (G-SIBs), which significantly expanded dollar credit. The overstretched nature of gross balance sheets denominated in the dollar at G-SIBs was attributed to changes in both the credit demand side and the credit supply side in the US shadow banking system during this period; these contributed to both the US housing bubble (2004–06) and the structural demand of the dollar-denominated safe, short-term, and liquid instruments.[1]

First of all, the US housing bubble led G-SIBs to hold 'excess capacity' in their gross balance sheets denominated in the dollar.[2] The US experienced a euphoric economy called the US housing bubble from 2004 to 2006, when US housing prices surged rapidly. The environment led G-SIBs to have surplus equity, in that their equity was larger than the amount required to meet its Value-at-Risk (VAR) constraint, driven by the rising market values of assets during the period. In response to this excess capacity, G-SIBs actively adjusted their gross balance sheets denominated in the dollar in order to expand their overall size, rather than paying out the surplus equity in the form of higher dividends (Adrian and Shin [2010], pp.17–18; Shin [2010], pp.119–120). On the liability side, the rising values of privately issued debt securities functioning as collateral assets including MBSs, ABSs, and CDOs, issued by securitization, allowed G-SIBs to take on more short-term dollar financing in the wholesale funding market such as repos, thus leading to the further increase in leverage and risk-taking. On the asset side, G-SIBs purchased long-term private-label debt securities with triple A-rating whose underlying assets were located in the US housing market, especially the subprime mortgage market during the euphoric economy from 2004 to 2006. As a result,

DOI: 10.4324/9781003733959-8

gross balance sheets denominated in the dollar at G-SIBs expanded rapidly during the housing bubble.

In turn, the crucial question is how G-SIBs could attract larger amounts of cheaper short-term dollar financing that allowed them to rapidly expand their gross balance sheets denominated in the dollar. As Pozsar (2011) points out, there was virtually insatiable demand for dollar-denominated safe, short-term, and liquid financial instruments from the institutional cash pools (in short, the cash pools), whose size has increased since the 1990s. Institutional cash pools rose from $100 billion in 1990 to over $2.2 trillion at their peak in 2007 (Pozsar 2011, pp.5–6). The institutional cash pools sought to invest part of their abundant cash funds in the dollar-denominated safe, short-term, and liquid instruments alternatives to insured bank deposits. Nevertheless, there was an insufficient supply of short-term government-guaranteed instruments in comparison with the strong demand for dollar-denominated safe, short-term, and liquid instruments from the institutional cash pools. This shortage has been estimated as $1.1, $1.6, and $1.6 trillion in 2005, 2006, and 2007, respectively (Pozsar 2011, pp.9–10).

What was the response of G-SIBs to the structural shortage of the dollar-denominated safe, short-term, and liquid instruments? First, G-SIBs issued private-label US debt securities by securitization, which appeared to be nearly as safe as US Treasuries and US Agencies. Specifically, Wall Street financial institutions and large European banks could create further MBSs, ABSs, and CDOs, largely through the origination and securitization of risky and long-term subprime mortgages.[3] As a result, the gross issuance of global private-label securitization reached a peak of nearly $5 trillion in 2006 (IMF [2011], p.13).[4] Second, G-SIBs including dealer banks used these private-label US debt securities, issued by securitization, as collateral assets for global repo borrowing. The faster expansion of US private-label debt securities as collateral assets allowed G-SIBs to accommodate credit demand for the dollar-denominated safe, short-term, and liquid instruments such as repos from the institutional cash pools, enabling G-SIBs to raise cheaper short-term dollar borrowing during the US housing bubble. In short, the faster expansion of US private-label debt securities, issued by securitization, as collateral assets during the US housing bubble allowed G-SIBs to raise cheaper short-term dollar borrowing, thus facilitating the rapid expansion of USD-denominated gross balance sheets at G-SIBs in the 2000s prior to the GFC.

2 The endogenously highly elastic finance of the global dollar in the shadow banking system

Notably, the volume of short-term dollar financing by G-SIBs in the shadow banking system was much bigger than the size of excess demand for the dollar-denominated short-term instruments from the institutional cash pools during US housing bubble. While the size of excess demand from the cash pools is estimated to be about \$1.6 trillion in 2007, secured funding operations reached \$10.0 trillion in that same year (Pozsar [2011], pp.9–10; Claessens et al. [2012], p.16). In order to accommodate the imbalance between credit supply and demand of secured funding, G-SIBs including dealer banks accelerated the supply of global dollars dynamically, allowing it to become more highly elastic.

Especially important in this respect, the intensive evolution of the global collateral plumbing at the central desk of dealer banks, central subsidiaries of G-SIBs, supported not only the mining and intermediating of collateral assets but also the reuse of collateral (i.e., rehypothecation), allowing G-SIBs to raise ever larger amounts of cheap short-term dollar borrowings (Singh 2011; European Commission 2013; Howell 2020).[5] Singh (2011) finds that the reuse of collateral allows the collateral to have 'velocity'. Similar to the velocity of money, the velocity of collateral—defined as the ratio between primary source collateral and total collateral received—supported multiple financial transactions in the shadow banking system. According to Figure 5.1, as of the end of 2007, the total collateral received by central collateral desks of banks and dealer banks was estimated to be \$10 trillion, and the primary sources of collateral from hedge funds (\$1.6) and securities lending (\$1.7) were \$3.3 trillion (\$1.6 plus \$1.7). Accordingly, the velocity of collateral is equal to about 3 (\$10 trillion/\$3.3 trillion).

The enhancement of the rehypothecation was partly conducted across geographical borders, which created 'the global rehypothecation chain of collateral' (Gupta [2021], p.20). As Gupta (2021) mentions, dealer banks typically maintained 'global settlement systems', in which dealers typically intermediate collateral from their US clients to their own foreign subsidiaries for internally borrowing dollar funding. This system was implemented by internally rehypothecating US client's collateral from dealer banks to their foreign siblings in offshore financial centers (OFCs) such as London where cheaper offshore Eurodollar funding was available.

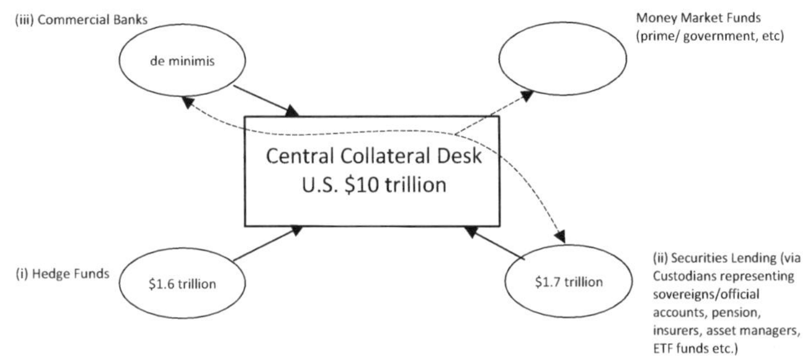

Figure 5.1 Pledged Collateral, 2007—Typical Sources and Uses

Source: Reproduced and revised from Singh (2011), p.5.

Note: Solid line indicates 'suppliers'. Dashed line indicates 'users'.

What attracted G-SIBs including dealer banks to depend largely on offshore Eurodollar borrowing in London? One of the main reasons is that the UK has not had rigid quantitative regulatory caps on collateral rehypothecation equivalent to those applicable to dealer banks regulated by the Securities and Exchange Commission (SEC) in the US. In the US, the SEC Rule 15c3-3 prevents dealer banks from using its customer's securities to finance its proprietary activities. Under this rule, dealer banks may use/rehypothecate an amount up to 140 percent of the customer's debt balance. By contrast, there was no limit on rehypothecation in the UK, attracting G-SIBs to rely on the reuse of collateral used in OFCs (Singh [2020], pp.18–19), which allowed them to expand their gross balance sheets denominated in the dollar. As a consequence, US banks and large European banks achieved a collateral multiplication of 400 percent, amounting to roughly $4.5 trillion in additional funding in London (Tooze [2018/2019], pp.81–82). Putting the pieces together, it could be interpreted that dynamics in global rehypothecation chain of collateral via OFCs contributed to G-SIBs endogenously creating the global dollar in the shadow banking system in the 2000s before the Global Financial Crisis of 2007–09.

Furthermore, a procyclical mechanism in the USD-denominated gross balance sheets at G-SIBs during the US housing bubble contributed to G-SIBs expanding rapidly short-term cheaper dollar borrowing through repos, overstretching their gross balance sheets denominated in the dollar. A stylized example of the procyclical mechanism in European banks' USD-denominated gross balance sheets is illustrated in Figure 5.2.

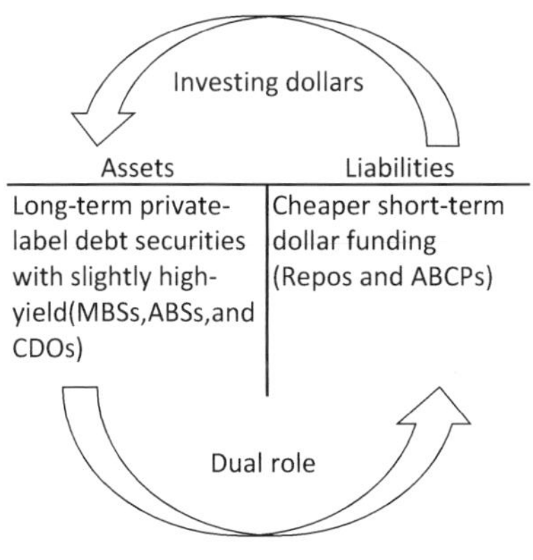

Figure 5.2 A Stylized T-Account of the Procyclical Mechanism of European Banks' USD-Denominated Gross Balance Sheets during the US Housing Bubble

Sources: Own elaboration on Adrian and Shin (2010), pp.18–19; Cömert (2013), pp.77–78.

Notes: MBSs = mortgage-backed securities; ABSs = asset-backed securities; CDOs = collateralized debt obligations; Repos = repurchase agreements; ABCPs = asset-backed commercial papers.

Long-term US private-label debt securities, which were created through securitization, played a dual role in USD-denominated gross balance sheets of European banks.[6] US private-label debt securities were used as collateral assets to raise short-term cheaper dollar borrowing through repos. G-SIBs subsequently used the dollars to invest again in long-term US private-label debt securities. The US housing bubble encouraged G-SIBs to amplify the self-expansion mechanism of their USD-denominated gross balance sheets, which provided G-SIBs with excessive leverage.[7] For instance, the level of leverage at European banks reached more than 45 times equity at its peak, whereas the level of leverage at US dealer banks and US commercial banks amounted to more than 30 times and 15 times, respectively, in the 2000s prior to the GFC (Haldane [2010], Annex, p.7, Chart 24). Hence, the procyclical mechanism provided G-SIBs with excessive leverage, thus overstretching their USD-denominated gross balance sheets during the US housing bubble.[8]

Along with the dynamically overstretched nature of USD-denominated gross balance sheets at G-SIBs, the endogenous finance of the global dollar in the shadow banking system became highly elastic in the run-up to the GFC. Figure 5.3 illustrates the outstanding external liabilities to foreigners by US financial institutions relative to the size of world GDP since Nixon Shock in 1971, when the US dollar-centric international monetary system transformed from the gold-dollar standard system under the BW system into the US dollar standard system in the floating exchange rate system.

Although the figure's time-series data contains all types of US financial institutions' external liabilities, it can be used as a proxy of the growth of global dollar supply from the US financial system, including US shadow banking

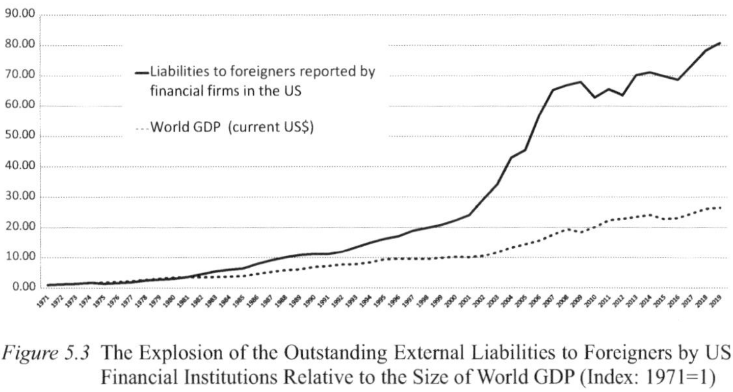

Figure 5.3 The Explosion of the Outstanding External Liabilities to Foreigners by US Financial Institutions Relative to the Size of World GDP (Index: 1971=1)

Sources: Own estimation on Board of Governors of Federal Reserve System, *Federal Reserve Bulletin*, various issues; World Bank database.

Notes: Before December 2013, reporting firms include all types of depository institutions as well as some bank holding companies and brokers and dealers. In addition, data include all other nonbank financial firms since December 2013, excluding bonds and notes of maturities longer than one year.

system, to the rest of the world in the long run. The volume of global dollar supply from US financial institutions vis-à-vis nonresidents had moderately increased until the late 1990s, amounting to 22.29 in 2000. Most surprisingly, it skyrocketed in the 2000s, especially during the US housing bubble, reaching from 34.15 in 2003 to more than 65.28 in 2007, while the size of world GDP increased from 11.38 to 17.63, respectively. As such, the explosion of global dollar creation from the US financial system during the US housing bubble implies that the endogenous finance of the global dollar supply in the shadow banking system became highly elastic during the housing bubble.

Overall, the endogenously highly elastic finance of the global dollar in the shadow banking system during the US housing bubble allowed the dynamic process of gross balance sheet expansions denominated in the dollar at G-SIBs.

3 The Global Financial Crisis of 2007–09

Conversely, the procyclical mechanism reversed since the GFC. For instance, the lower level of haircuts/margins of US private-label debt securities before the GFC rose sharply during the GFC. The haircuts/margins of even prime MBSs (single A- and double A-rated) and triple A-rated structured assets soared to 100 percent in June 2009 from 8–10 percent in June 2007 (CGFS [2010], p.2). This means that a large portion of US private-label debt securities, issued by securitization, were no longer accepted as collateral assets, which enabled G-SIBs to raise cheaper short-term dollar borrowing in the repo markets, once the euphoric expectations of the US housing bubble ended. The sudden and sharp fall in the US private-label debt securities as collateral assets precipitated a sudden disappearance of short-term global dollar borrowings at G-SIBs. The sudden change, in turn, triggered a drastic contraction of USD-denominated gross balance sheets at G-SIBs during the global financial crisis. It can be identified that the heightened pressures in short-term global dollar funding in US repo markets forced G-SIBs to deleverage their gross balance sheet (liabilities plus assets) denominated in the dollar in the midst of the GFC, in the following quotation from a report on the second quarter of 2008 of US international transactions from the Survey of Current Business published by the US Bureau of Economic Analysis (BEA).

> The decrease resulted from decreases in the liabilities of securities brokers and dealers (dealer banks: author) and banks, particularly of foreign-owned institutions (European banks: author) in the United States. Brokers' and dealers' liabilities, mostly repurchase agreements, decreased especially sharply. The decrease coincided with a decrease in brokers' and dealers' claims, as these highly leveraged institutions sought to reduce their international borrowing and lending.
>
> (Hoang and Whitaker [2008], p.72)

All in all, the endogenously highly elastic finance of the global dollar in the shadow banking system during the US housing bubble accelerated the dynamically overstretched nature of gross balance sheets denominated in the dollar at G-SIBs. By contrast, the collapse of US private-label debt securities, issued by securitization, triggered the sudden disappearance of the endogenous financing of the global dollar in the shadow banking system at the height of the GFC of 2007–09, thus leading to the rapid deleveraging of gross balance sheets denominated in the dollar at G-SIBs. As a result, gross capital flows dropped drastically from 43.2 percent in 2007 to 5.32 percent in 2008 and then 4.9 percent in 2009, which almost matched the volume of net capital flows (3.61 percent in 2009) (See Figure 1.2).

Therefore, it can be concluded that the US dollar standard system centered around the shadow banking system has a dynamic and ultimately destructive nature in the 2000s.

Notes

1 Part of the material in Chapter 5 was drawn on Tokunaga and Epstein (2018) and Tokunaga (2019).
2 Adrian and Shin (2010); Shin (2010); Cömert (2013).
3 Awrey (2012) describes that the securitization enabled G-SIBs to "make new assets out of thin air" (p.33).
4 Furthermore, two mechanisms also sustained securitization based on subprime mortgages. First, high credit ratings allowed G-SIBs to successfully sell US debt securities, which were securitized from subprime mortgage loans to other investors (White 2009). Second, G-SIBs bought large amounts of credit default swaps (CDSs) on ABSs and CDOs, written by insurance companies such as American International Group (AIG), which hedged the credit risk associated with the underlying assets: the subprime mortgages (IMF [2011], p.9).
5 The rehypothecation of collateral assets is also important in derivatives trading. Based on ISDA (2015), it is likely that a large part of cash denominated in the US dollar and US government bonds are actually reused in derivatives.
6 The dual role of US securities in the expansion of USD-denominated gross balance sheets at G-SIBs allows them to use the securities as collateral assets: while US securities serves as eligible assets with a relatively higher yield on the asset side, they were also used as collateral assets to supply new financial instruments (e.g., repos) with a relatively higher yield alternative to insured deposits on the liability side (Mehrling [2011], p.92; Gordon and Metric [2012], pp.24–27, 51; Bayoumi and Bui [2012], p.8).
7 Cömert (2013) is a pioneering study explaining how the endogenously self-expansion mechanism of balance sheets at financial institutions led to a financial explosion during the US housing bubble.
8 Similarly, some literature also suggests characteristics of the mechanism: positive feedback effect (CGFS 2011) and feedback loop (ESRB 2014).

References

Adrian, T. and H.S. Shin (2010), "The Changing Nature of Financial Intermediation and the Financial Crisis of 2007–2009", *Federal Reserve Bank of New York Staff Reports*, no.439, March 2010.

Awrey, D. (2012), Toward a Supply-Side Theory of Financial Innovation, June 27, 2012, Available at SSRN: https://ssrn.com/abstract=2094254

Bayoumi, T. and T. Bui (2012), "Apocalypse Then: The Evolution of the North Atlantic Economy and the Global Crisis", *IMF Working Paper*, International Monetary Fund (IMF), 11/212, September 2011.

Claessens S., Z. Pozsar, L. Ratnovski, and M. Singh (2012), "Shadow Banking: Economics and Policy", *Staff Discussion*, International Monetary Fund (IMF), December 4, 2012.

Cömert, H. (2013), *Central Banks and Financial Markets: The Declining Power of US Monetary Policy*, Cheltenham and Northampton: Edward Elgar.

Committee on the Global Financial System (CGFS) (2010), The Role of Margin Requirements and Haircuts in Procyclicality, *CGFS Papers*, Bank for International Settlements (BIS), no.36, March 2010.

Committee on the Global Financial System (CGFS) (2011), Global Liquidity Concept, Measurement and Policy Implication, *CGFS Papers*, Bank for International Settlements (BIS), no.45, November 2011.

European Commission (2013), *Shadow Banking-Addressing New Sources of Risk in the Financial Sector*, Brussels, 4.9.2013 COM (2013) 614 final, European Commission, September 4, 2013.

European Systemic Risk Board (ESRB) (2014), *Is Europe Overbanked? Reports of the Advisory Scientific Committee*, European Systemic Risk Board (ESRB), no.4, June 2014.

Gorton, G. and A. Metrick (2012), "Securitization", *NBER Working Paper*, National Bureau of Economic Research (NBER), no.18611, December 2012.

Gupta, A. (2021), "The Internal Capital Markets of Global Dealer Banks", *Finance and Economics Discussion Series*, Board of Governors of the Federal Reserve System, 2021-036, June 7, 2021.

Haldane, A. (2010), "The Contribution of the Financial Sector: Miracle or Mirage?" Paper Presented at the Future of Finance Conference, London, Bank of England (BOE), July 14, 2010.

Hoang, M.-C. and E.M. Whitaker (2008), "US International Transactions Second Quarter of 2008", *Survey of Current Business*, US Bureau of Economic Analysis (BEA), October 2008, pp.64–73.

Howell, M.J. (2020), *Capital Wars: The Rise of Global Liquidity*, Basingstoke: Palgrave Macmillan.

International Monetary Fund (IMF) (2011), The Multilateral Aspects of Policies Affecting Capital Flows: Background Paper, International Monetary Fund (IMF), October 21, 2011.

International Swaps and Derivatives Association (ISDA) (2015), ISDA Margin Survey 2015, International Swaps and Derivatives Association (ISDA), August 2015.

Mehrling, P. (2011), *The New Lombard Street: How the Fed Became the Dealer of Last Resort*, Princeton, NJ: Princeton University Press.

Pozsar, Z. (2011), "Institutional Cash Pools and the Triffin Dilemma of the US Banking System", *IMF Working Paper*, International Monetary Fund (IMF), 11/190, August 2011.

Shin, H.S. (2010), *Risk and Liquidity*, New York: Oxford University Press.

Singh, M. (2011), "Velocity of Pledged Collateral: Analysis and Implications", *IMF Working Paper*, International Monetary Fund (IMF), 11/256, November 2011.

Singh, M. (2020), *Collateral Markets and Financial Plumbing*, Third Edition, London: Risk Books.

Tokunaga, J. (2019), "The Comparative Advantage of the US Shadow Banking System and the Role of the US Dollar", *The Japanese Political Economy*, vol.45, issue 1–2, pp.20–42.

Tokunaga, J. and G. Epstein (2018), "The Endogenous Finance of Global-Dollar-Based Financial Fragility in the 2000s: A Minskyan Approach", *Review of Keynesian Economics*, vol.6, issue 1, pp.62–82.

Tooze, A. (2018/2019), *Crashed: How a Decade of Financial Crises Changed the World*, London: Penguin Books.

White, L.J. (2009), The Credit Rating Agencies and the Subprime Debacle, *Critical Review*, vol.21, issue 2–3, pp.389–399.

Part IV

The present structure of the US dollar standard system

6 The unparalleled status of US Treasury securities as collateral assets in the 2010s

1 The evolution in the US Fed role as lender of last resort during the GFC

As shown in Figure 1.2, gross capital flows plummeted from 43.2 percent in 2007 to 4.9 percent in 2009, which largely reflected that global systemically important banks (G-SIBs) rapidly shrank their gross balance sheets denominated in the dollar amid the Global Financial Crisis (GFC) of 2007–09. If G-SIBs' gross balance sheets denominated in the dollar collapsed entirely, there might be, ceteris paribus, the panicked dollar's sell-off and the terrified US capital outflow in some cases. Considering that the US was the epicenter of the GFC, the dollar standard system might have been near collapse at the height of the financial crisis.

But the opposite happened. The 'flight to quality' led to larger capital inflows into the US Treasury markets as safe haven and appreciation of the dollar exchange rate. This implies that the dollar standard system survived somehow, enabling G-SIBs to avoid the entire collapse of their gross balance sheets activity denominated in the dollar in the outbreak of the GFC. What allowed G-SIBs to get off the hook?

One of the major institutional frameworks was in the US Federal Reserve (Fed)'s monetary policy, in which it extended its role as a lender of last resort (LLR) to alleviate dollar shortages at G-SIBs, especially European banks, during the GFC. As documented by many studies, the development of Fed monetary policy measures for countering the GFC was marked by three phases: (1) the subprime mortgage crisis in summer of 2007, (2) the collapse of Bear Stearns in March 2008, and (3) the failure of Lehman Brothers and American International Group (AIG) in September 2008. In the first phase of the crisis, the Fed took standard measures such as the reductions in policy interest rates (i.e., federal funds rates) to alleviate the financial panic since the subprime crisis in summer of 2007, which reached the effective zero lower bound in December 2008. The Fed also set up various extensions of discount window facilities to support distressed banks facing the dollar shortage. The list of the largest financial institutions of the discount window in 2008 included not only large US banks but also European banks (Tooze [2018/2019], p.207).

DOI: 10.4324/9781003733959-10

Furthermore, in response to the collapse of asset-backed commercial papers (ABCPs) markets in the autumn of 2007, the Fed introduced new discount window credit called the Term Auction Facility (TAF), which provided banks facing the dollar shortage with access to short-term dollar funds. Among the large borrowers, the foreign share was over 50 percent (Tooze [2018/2019], p.207). In short, the development of the Fed's discount window for not only US financial institutions but also non-US banks, mainly European banks, means that the Fed played a traditional role of the LLR in the first phase of the crisis.

Following the bankruptcy of Bear Stearns in March 2008, the financial crisis entered the second phase, in which the dollar liquidity crunch happened suddenly in the US repo market, driven by the outbreak of "run on repo" (Gorton and Metrick 2012a). In response, the Fed deployed a series of nonstandard monetary policy measures by "using every weapon at hand, including a number of new ones never used before" (Mehrling [2011], p.1). Specifically, the Fed set in motion the Term Securities Lending Facility (TSLF), which allowed US primary dealers to borrow US Treasury securities as collateral assets on a 28-day term in exchange for a variety of private-label MBSs. In total, $2 trillion in safest collateral assets (i.e., US Treasury securities) was injected into the financial system through this facility. Of the collateral assets supplied by the TSLF, 51 percent was provided to non-US banks, with Royal Bank of Scotland, Deutsche Bank, and Credit Suisse alone obtaining over $800 billion (Tooze [2018/2019], p.208). At the same time, the Fed initiated the Primary Dealer Credit Facility (PDCF) as the largest backstop for US repo markets, which provided overnight loans to US primary dealers through their clearing banks (i.e., Bank of New York Mellon and JP Morgan Chase), in exchange for a wide range of eligible collateral assets. The PDCF supported not only US financial institutions but also the London-based subsidiaries of Goldman Sachs, Morgan Stanley, Merrill Lynch, and Citigroup which used the program (Tooze [2018/2019], pp.208–209). Thus, in the second phase of the crisis, the Fed extended its function of the LLR over US commercial banks in the traditional banking system directly to US dealer banks and European banks in the shadow banking system, thus setting itself up as a "dealer of last resort" (Mehrling 2011).

In the third phase, in response to the dollar shortage in the global and offshore dimension, on December 2007 the Fed took an initiative to temporarily establish foreign exchange swap lines with foreign central banks. The swap network comprising the US Fed, the European Central Bank (ECB), Bank of Japan (BOJ), Bank of England (BOE), Swiss National Bank (SNB), and Bank of Canada (BOC) is often called 'C6'. ECB lent out dollar funds, which were provided by the Fed through the swap lines, into European banks facing the dollar shortage. The G6 swap network was made permanent and unlimited in October 2013 (Murau, Pape and Pforr [2022], pp.8–10). As such, in the third phase of the crisis, the Fed extended its role as LLR into the global and offshore sphere.

All in all, the evolution of the Fed's role as LLR, which was followed by its three times' quantitative easing (QE) programs starting in December 2008, not only supplied massive dollar liquidity to G-SIBs facing the dollar shortage but also exchanged the private-label US debt securities that were unacceptable as collateral assets with US Treasury securities as safest collateral. In this sense, the evolution of the Fed's role as LLR could backstop G-SIBs to prevent the further shrinking of their gross balance sheets denominated in the dollar in the face of the GFC. As a result, the volume of gross capital flows bottomed out from 4.9 percent in 2009 to 19.3 percent in 2010 (Figure 1.2).

2 The intensification in the structural shortage of global safe assets in the 2010s

As Figure 1.2 shows, the volume of gross capital flows hovered around 10 percent and 15 percent for most of the 2010s, which remained below their pre-GFC trend. Given the US dollar's dominance in international financial markets (Figure 1.1), most gross capital flows were still denominated in the dollar in the 2010s, which largely reflected that G-SIBs denominated their gross balance sheets in the dollar. As described in the beginning of Chapter 3.1, the shortage of global safe assets was one deep-rooted cause of facilitating G-SIBs to expand their gross balance sheets before the GFC of 2007–09. How did the shortage of global safe assets change in the 2010s?

Governments in advanced countries ramped up their fiscal deficits to shore up the distressed financial markets and to stimulate the economy during the GFC of 2007–09 and the Great Recession. In the US, growing federal deficits caused outstanding marketable US Treasury securities to increase from $4,494 billion at the end of 2007 to $11.834 billion at the end of 2013.[1] As a result, the stock of US government debts as global safe assets (ratio to global GDP) rose from 9.2 percent in 2007 to 15.8 percent in 2011.[2] Nevertheless, larger portions of US private-label debt securities including asset-backed securities (ABSs), as well as EU peripheral government debt, were no longer accepted as safe assets since the GFC. Consequently, the outstanding total gross safe assets (ratio to global GDP) shrunk considerably from 51.5 percent in 2007 to 37.7 percent in 2011.[3] In short, the supply of global safe assets was still inadequate in the 2010s.

In comparison with the inefficient supply of global safe assets, the structural demand for global safe assets was amplified further by the advent of 'the age of asset management' in the 2010s (Haldane 2014). According to Willis Towers Watson, total investment funds under management by the world's top 17 assets management firms with more than $1 trillion was more than $41.1 trillion in early 2017 (Epstein [2019], p.9). These asset managers can be called 'the Giants of International Capitalism', who invest their funds in the market with the expectation of above-average returns (Phillips [2018], p.35). In particular, the largest three US asset managers (BlackRock, Vanguard, and State Street), as well as G-SIBs in the US and Europe, are ranked highly in the top 17 asset managers in early 2017 (Phillips [2018], p.37). The rise of assets management accelerated, to a greater extent, the structural demand for global safe assets in the 2010s. Overall, due to the increasing imbalances between supply and demand for safe assets, the structural shortage of global safe assets intensified in the 2010s.

Could the shadow banking system on both sides of the Atlantic respond to the structural shortage of global safe assets in the 2010s? In the next two sections (Sections 3 and 4), we analyze whether or not the shadow banking system on both sides of the Atlantic could adequately fulfill its two important functions, i.e., securitization and collateral intermediation for responding to the increased shortage of global safe assets in the 2010s.

3 The less developed dynamics in the US shadow banking system in the 2010s

Since the GFC, G-SIBs pulled back from their global ALM strategy based on the originate-to-distribute (OTD) model which expanded their gross balance sheets denominated in the dollar in the 2000s prior to the financial crisis.

On the one hand, the strengthening of regulation and oversight on the OTD model led G-SIBs to drastically reduce securitization activity since the GFC. As Adrian (2017) points out, the increase in regulation and oversight includes the strengthening of loan underwriting standards; the expanded scope of prudential consolidation requiring banks who sponsor off-balance sheet vehicles to hold regulatory capital against these exposures; the increase in information disclosure requirements; and the adaptation of credit retention requirements to better align the incentives of originators and investors. Against this backdrop, the issuance of US MBSs based on subprime mortgage loans almost ceased (Adrian 2017).

On the other hand, the changes in monetary policy and the stricter capital and liquidity regulation on banks since the GFC facilitated G-SIBs to drain high-quality and liquid government bonds functioning as collateral assets, which undermined the space of collateral intermediation in the 2010s. First, the implementation of quantitative easing (QE) and bond-buying under asset purchase programs by central banks in advanced countries absorbed a large part of government bonds serving as collateral assets from G-SIBs' gross balance sheets since the GFC. Second, the introduction of new financial regulations led G-SIBs to silo high-quality and liquid sovereign bonds called 'High-Quality Liquid Assets' (HQLAs) on their own balance sheets. Regulators introduced capital requirements and reform for G-SIBs, set by the Dodd-Frank Act and Basel III by the Basel Committee on Banking Supervision (BCBS).

One of the most critical post-crisis regulatory reforms which reshaped the dynamics of collateral intermediation is the Basel III reform, which includes the Liquidity Coverage Ratio (LCR) and the Net Stable Funding Ratio (NSFR). Especially, the LCR requires banks to hold a sufficient reserve of HQLAs including US Treasury bonds to allow them to survive a period of significant liquidity stress lasting 30 calendar days.[4] Against this backdrop, as of September 2014, of the aggregate supply of high-quality collateral estimated to be $42 trillion, the unencumbered and available supply of high-quality collateral was only $8.5 trillion (Baranova, Liu and Noss [2016], p,5).

The drain of government bonds as collateral assets, combined with the withdrawal of OTD model at G-SIBs, altered the structure of global collateral plumbing in the 2010s. Singh (2020) distinguishes the 'new' collateral space in the 2010s from the 'old' collateral space in the 2000s before the GFC. In the old collateral space, the pledged collateral assets were typically intermediated by the central collateral desk of banks and dealers, which reused the collateral to meet the demand (Figure 5.1). However, the shortage of government bonds as collateral assets, led by the changes in monetary policy and the stricter capital and liquidity regulation, resulted in the emergence of new collateral space, where other participants, including central banks and collateral custodians, gained importance in collateral intermediation in the 2010s.

The new collateral space, combined with the failures (e.g., Lehman Brothers) and mergers (e.g., Bear Stearns and Merrill Lynch) of US dealer banks during the GFC, put many strains on the efficient functioning of global collateral plumbing. The lacks in dynamics of global collateral plumbing, in turn, led to the drastic decrease in the reuse (i.e., rehypothecation) at the central collateral desk of banks and dealer banks in the 2010s. After the rate in velocity of collateral reached a peak of 3.0 in 2007 (volume of pledged collateral $10.0 trillion/primary collateral sources $3.3 trillion) (Singh [2011], p.13), the rate dropped to only 1.8 (volume of pledged collateral $6.1 trillion/primary collateral sources $3.3 trillion) in 2016 (Singh [2020], Table 2.3, p.37). As a result, total US repo activity dropped by almost half from $10 trillion at its pre-crisis peak to around $5 trillion in the post-crisis era (Baklanova, Copeland and McCaughrin [2015], p.1).

Instead of depending on the OTD model, G-SIBs migrated into a new type of ALM model for pursuing higher sustainable profitability in the 2010s (Caparusso et al. 2019). As far as the US shadow banking system is concerned, G-SIBs swiftly increased other activities including collateralized loan obligations (CLOs) and exchange-traded funds (ETFs) (Adrian 2017). In particular, the outstanding US CLOs, which are structured private-label debt securities backed primarily by pools of leveraged loans, grew dramatically from $264 billion in 2011 to $617 billion in 2018 (Guse et al. 2019).

CLOs-related securitization activities are deeply linked to offshore financial centers (OFCs), in the sense that US CLOs are typically structured as special purpose vehicles (SPVs) in OFCs, especially the Cayman Islands, benefiting from regulatory arbitrage and tax avoidance. At the end of 2018, around $457 billion (74 percent) of US CLO securities were issued out of the Cayman Islands, and of these Cayman issues, $409 billion (89 percent) were held by US investors (Liu and Schmidt-Eisenlohr 2019/2020). The round-tripping transactions of US CLOs' activities between the US shadow banking system and Caribbean financial centers contributed, in part, to the resilience of gross balance sheets denominated in the dollar at G-SIBs in the 2010s.

Nevertheless, the growth of securitization in the US in the 2010s did not recover to pre-GFC level. The US leveraged loan markets, which were largely structured and funded by the issuance of US CLOs, were in absolute term half the size of the subprime mortgage markets at its peak in the 2000s before the GFC (Adrian 2017). Additionally, while US Treasury securities have the largest position as collateral assets, the role of CLOs as collateral seems to be marginal, hindering the efficient functioning of collateral intermediation in the 2010s.

Thus, the US shadow banking system lacked more dynamics in the 2010s than pre-GFC level, in that it could not fully fulfill two important functions, i.e., securitization and collateral intermediation, in the 2010s.

4 The underdevelopment of the shadow banking system in the Eurozone in the 2010s

The Eurozone faced considerable scarcity of government bonds as safe assets in the 2010s. First, the inefficient supply of euro-denominated sovereign bonds as safe assets was driven by the Eurozone debt crisis in 2011–13. Before the GFC of 2007–09, market participants regarded sovereign bonds of peripheral member countries (including Greece) as almost equivalent to the safest assets in the Eurozone, i.e., Germany bonds. With the outbreak of the Eurozone debt crisis, government bonds from the peripheral countries lost their standings as safe assets. According to credit ratings in the Eurozone countries, though there were eight triple-A-rated governments in 2007, the debt crisis decreased the number of the highest ratings to only three (Germany, Luxembourg, and the Netherlands) in 2015 (Bogołębska, Feder-Sempach and Stawasz-Grabowska [2024], pp.147–148). Second, ECB bond-buying under the public sector purchase program (PSPP) for quantitative easing (QE) introduced in March 2015 absorbed a large amount of high-rated government bonds in the Eurozone. The Eurosystem holdings accounted for about 20 percent of total public debts in the Eurozone on December 2018 when the PSPP was finished, which was twice the share of the US Federal Reserve System holding of government bonds of total public debts in the US (Eichengreen and Gros [2020], p.29). As a result, the stock of triple A-rated debt securities in the Eurozone declined from around 40 percent of its GDP in 2008 to around 20 percent in 2018 (Claeys and Wolff [2020], p.5).

In spite of the inefficient supply of government bonds available for safe assets in the Eurozone in the 2010s, there remained a rising demand for not only high-rated sovereign bonds in member states but also alternative privately created debt securities denominated in the euro as safe assets. Could the shadow banking system in the Eurozone respond to the structural shortage of safe assets denominated in the euro in the 2010s? On the one hand, new issuance of privately securitized assets in the Eurozone plummeted to below €200 billion in 2013 after having topped out at over €700 billion in 2008 (ESRB [2023], Annex, Chart A27, p.24). Similar to US securitization activities in the 2010s, European CLOs issuance resumed in tandem with a rise in the leveraged loan market since 2013. But the total outstanding European CLOs in the EU remain much smaller than the US (ESRB [2023], pp.60–61). In order to revive the securitization activity, the EU set in motion a new framework for simple, transparent, and standardized (STS) securitization on multiple levels. But it was unclear that the STS could stabilize the securitization markets (Kirschenmann, Riedler and Schuler 2018, p.7; Lannoo and Thomadakis 2019, p.20). Against this backdrop, the issuance of European securitization remained sluggish, between €200 billion and €300 billion in the 2010s (ESRB [2023], Annex, Chart A27, p.24).

On the other hand, similar to the stagnation of securitization activities, the Eurozone-wide collateral intermediation was still underdeveloped in the 2010s. First, EU government bonds functioning as collateral assets were less important than US Treasury securities within the EU. The European Systemic Risk Board (ESRB) conducted the first comprehensive survey of securities financing transactions such as repos in Europe in the first half of the 2010s. As of the end of February 2013, the volume of collateral received was €3,971 billion and collateral posted €4,576 billion. In the collateral category, government bonds (82 percent) were the largest collateral assets received and posted by reporting entities, of which US government debts accounted for the largest share (20 percent), followed by the UK (14 percent), Germany (14 percent), and France (9 percent) (Keller et al. [2014], pp.13–14). Second, European repo markets are still regulated by member state laws, which are subject to varying degrees of harmonization at the EU level (Wu and Nabilou 2018). Lastly, many barriers for cross-border collateral mobilization remained within the Eurozone (ECB [2014], pp.6–7), impeding the efficient process for cross-border collateral intermediation. Taken together, these flaws in collateral intermediation partly hindered the development of European repo markets for a few years in the aftermath of the Eurozone debt crisis. The outstandings of the European repo market (repo plus reverse repo positions) decreased rapidly from the peak of €6,775 billion in June 2007 to €4,633 in December 2008, and thereafter the volume levelled off at between €5,000 and €6,000 until the end of 2016.[5] Hence, the shadow banking system in the Eurozone continued to be underdeveloped in the 2010s, in that it could not fulfill two important functions, i.e., securitization and collateral intermediation.[6]

Overall, the shadow banking system on both sides of the Atlantic could not adequately fulfill its two important functions, i.e., securitization and collateral intermediation in the 2010s, as it was unable to respond to the intensified structural shortage of global safe assets.

5 The US Treasury securities as universal collateral assets in the 2010s

Since the shadow banking system on both sides of the Atlantic could not respond to the intensified structural shortage of global safe assets in the 2010s, the structural scarcity of global safe assets was largely filled by the unrivaled position of US Treasury securities as safe assets relative to those of the Eurozone in the 2010s.[7] Eichengreen and Gros (2020) demonstrate the outstanding government bonds available to the broader financial markets in the US and the Eurozone, excluding the holdings of central banks or commercial banks, at the end of 2008 when the US Fed started quantitate easing (QE); the end of 2014 when the Fed ended its bond-buying under the asset purchase program and the ECB had not yet begun the public sector purchase program (PSPP); and the end of 2019 just after the end of the PSPP by the ECB. The supply of US Treasury bonds as safe assets was 3.23 times larger than that of the Eurozone ($7,926 billion/$2,455 billion) in 2008, and the ratio increased to 3.60 times in 2014 ($13,088 billion/$3,636 billion) and reached 5.83 times ($16,827/$2,885) in 2019.[8]

What underpins the unparalleled role of US Treasuries as safe assets in the world in the 2010s? Of particular importance is the structural demand for US Treasury securities from both US domestic and foreign investors in all market conditions. To explain the insatiable demand for US Treasury bonds, Hager (2016, 2017) suggests 'the powerful bond of interest between US domestic and foreign investors of US public debts': the top 1 percent of US households invest heavily in US Treasury securities either directly or indirectly through its ownership of institutional investors, which alleviates foreigners' concerns about the creditworthiness of growing US federal deficits. Meanwhile, the richest US domestic owners benefit from foreign demand for US Treasury bonds, thus helping to deflect taxes on the top 1 percent of US households.

Especially important, the significant presence of foreign official holdings of US Treasury securities supported the powerful bond of interest between US domestic and foreign owners of US Treasury securities in the GFC of 2007–09. During the GFC, US Treasuries as safe haven strongly attracted foreign official investors. Foreign central banks in East Asia, especially China, accumulated US Treasury securities as their foreign exchange reserves in the midst of the GFC. While the outstanding US Treasury securities held by Japan increased from $622.9 billion in June 2007 to $882.3 billion in December 2010, China's holding of US Treasuries rose rapidly from $477.3 billion to

1,160.1 billion, respectively.[9] As a result, China surpassed Japan to become the largest holder of US Treasury bonds during that period. Hung (2016) calls China's insatiable demand for the US Treasury securities "China's addiction to US Treasuries". As such, the powerful bond of interests between US domestic and foreign owners of US Treasury securities shored up the structural demand for US Treasury securities in the 2010s.

Notably, the seemingly permanent demand for US Treasury bonds enables the US Treasury markets to function as the largest, deepest, and most liquid markets in the world, which allows US domestic and foreign investors to purchase or sell US Treasuries quickly in all market conditions without causing a drastic change in the securities' prices, thereby nourishing market liquidity in the Treasury markets. The bigger market liquidity in US Treasury markets, the greater the demand for US Treasury bonds from a broad range of market participants worldwide to buy or sell, increasing further market liquidity in the Treasury markets. This self-enforcing mechanism of market liquidity in the Treasury markets eventually enables US Treasury securities to play an unrivaled role as the safest assets in the world.

Given the unparalleled position of US Treasury securities as the safest assets, G-SIBs including dealer banks use US Treasury bonds as collateral assets in US repo markets. Though there lacked quantitative data for verifying the role of US Treasuries as collateral assets before the GFC of 2007–09, US monetary authorities have conducted some pilot investigations by collecting pieces of data of the repos and securities lending in the US since the 2010s.[10] Among other things, the Securities Industry and Financial Markets Association (SIFMA) (2022), the leading trade association for dealer banks and asset managers in the US, provides detailed data of the collateral asset category in US repo markets as of December 9, 2021. US Treasury securities accounted for the largest share of collateral assets in all segments of US repo markets. In the bilateral repo market, average daily outstandings amounted to $2.5 trillion, of which the collateral asset class was Treasury securities 67.7 percent, while mortgage-backed security (MBS) was 15.6 percent and Treasuries inflation-protected securities (TIPS) 7.3 percent. In the bilateral reverse repo market, average daily outstanding reached $1.8 trillion, of which the collateral asset category was Treasury securities 79.3 percent, TIPS 9.7 percent, and MBS 9.6 percent. General collateral finance (GCF) repo average daily par amount was $78.5 billion, of which the collateral asset class was Treasury securities 63.7 percent and MBS 36.3 percent. In the tri-party repo markets, the collateral asset category was Treasury securities 70.1 percent and Agency MBS and collateralized mortgage obligations (CMOs) 18.0 percent.[11] Thus, US Treasury securities were recognized as universal collateral assets, which market participants worldwide used for repos in all market conditions in the 2010s.[12]

Given the universal status of US Treasury securities as collateral assets in the repo markets, G-SIBs including global dealer banks used US Treasuries as collateral for the endogenous financing of the global dollar in the shadow banking system in the 2010s. In global dollar repo markets, while daily transactions involving only US entities reached $2 trillion, daily deals involving a non-US entity were $1 trillion (CGFS [2020], Table 1, pp.12–13). The dynamics in the endogenous finance of the global dollar collateralized by US Treasury securities in the shadow banking system facilitated the resilience of gross balance sheets denominated in the dollar at G-SIBs in the 2010s. As a result, gross capital flows recovered but remained below their pre-GFC trend in the 2010s (hovering around 10 percent and 15 percent for the most part), though it fluctuated from year to year (Figure 1.2).[13]

Therefore, it can be interpreted that US Treasury securities functioned as universal collateral assets for the endogenous finance of the global dollar in the shadow banking system, which helped G-SIBs to expand their gross balance sheets denominated in the dollar in the 2010s.

Notes

1 Data from Board of Governors of the Federal Reserve System, Flow of Funds of the United States.
2 Davies (2020).
3 Davies (2020).
4 The additional demands stemming from the Dodd-Frank Act and Basel III for collateral assets such as US Treasury securities are estimated at about $2–4 trillion (Singh [2020], p.144).
5 Data from the International Capital Market Association European Repo Market Survey website.
6 In addition, as referred to in Chapter 3.5.1, it is imperative for the ECB to play the role of the LLR for tackling Eurozone-wide crises such as the Eurozone debt crisis of 2011–13. After a series of the extend and pretend monetary policy by the ECB at the outset of the Eurozone debt crisis, the bank established the Outright Monetary Transactions (OMT) in September 2013, under which the bank purchases sovereign bonds issued by Eurozone member states in secondary markets. Though the announcement of the OMT worked to abate the Eurozone debt crisis, the role of the ECB playing the role of the LLR through the OMT was strictly conditional (Tooze 2018/2019, p.441), unlike the unconditional purchase programs of US Treasury bonds by the US Fed. In this sense, the ECB still had a major institutional flaw in fulfilling the role of the LLR in tackling the Eurozone-wide crises, compared to the US Fed, in the 2010s.
7 It has been widely recognized that the unparalleled status of US Treasury securities as safe assets play the following crucial roles in global financial markets: collateral assets for repos, collaterals for securities lending; collaterals for derivatives, benchmarks in international capital markets, foreign exchange reserves held by monetary authorities, and safe haven in crisis (Schinasi, Kramer and Smith 2001; Gorton and Metrick 2012b; He, Krishnamurthy and Milbradt 2016; US Department of the Treasury, Board of Governors of the Federal Reserve System, Federal Reserve Bank of New York, US Securities and Exchange Commission, and US Commodity Futures Trading Commission 2015; Group of Thirty 2021; Ryan and Toomey 2021). In addition to the global sphere, US Treasury securities markets play important roles in fiscal and monetary policy in the US economy: the primary

means of financing the US federal government and important markets for the Federal Reserve's implementation of monetary policy.

8 Own calculations from the data from Eichengreen and Gros (2020), Table 4, p.28.

9 Data from the US Department of Treasury, Treasury International Capital (TIC) System website.

10 Baklanova (2015); Baklanova, Caglio, Cipriani and Copeland (2016); Baklanova, Caglio, Keane and Porter (2016); Infante, Press and Strauss (2018); Kahn and Olson (2021); Paddrik, Ramírez and McCormick (2021); Hempel et al. (2024).

11 Data from SIFMA (2022).

12 The role of US Treasury securities in repo markets is regarded as 'universally accepted collateral' (Schinasi, Kramer and Smith [2001], pp.4–5) or 'the most sought-after collateral assets' (Awrey [2017], p.975). In addition, Ryan and Toomey (2021) consider US Treasuries as "a bedrock of the global financial system".

13 Fostel, Geanakoplos, and Phelan (2019) explain that collateral-based financing innovations are an important driver of gross capital flows.

References

Adrian, T. (2017), *Shadow Banking and Market Based Finance, Helsinki*, International Monetary Fund (IMF), September 14, 2017.

Awrey, D. (2017), "Brother, Can You Spare a Dollar? Designing an Effective Framework for Foreign Currency Liquidity Assistance", *Columbia Business Law Review*, 934, pp.934–1016.

Baklanova, V. (2015), "Repo and Securities Lending: Improving Transparency with Better Data", *OFR Brief Series*, Office of Financial Research (OFR), 15-03, April 23, 2015.

Baklanova, V., C. Caglio, M. Cipriani, and A. Copeland (2016), "The US Bilateral Repo Market: Lessons from a New Survey", *OFR Working Paper*, Office of Financial Research (OFR), 16-01, January 23, 2016.

Baklanova, V., C. Caglio, F. Keane, and B. Porter (2016), "A Pilot Survey of Agent Securities Lending Activity", *OFR Working Paper*, Office of Financial Research (OFR), 16-08, August 23, 2016.

Baklanova, V., A. Copeland, and R. McCaughrin (2015), "Reference Guide to US Repo and Securities Lending Markets", *Federal Reserve Bank of New York Staff Report*, no.740, September 2015.

Baranova, Y., Liu, Z., and Noss, J. (2016), "The Role of Collateral in Supporting Liquidity", *Bank of England Working Papers*, Bank of England (BOE), no.609, August 2016.

Bogołębska, J., E. Feder-Sempach, and E. Stawasz-Grabowska (2024), *Safe Assets in the Global Economy: Supply, Demand and Financial Stability*, Abingdon: Routledge.

Caparusso, J., C.Y. Chen, P. Dattels, R. Goel, and P. Hiebert (2019), "Post-Crisis Changes in Global Bank Business Models: A New Taxonomy", *IMF Working Paper*, International Monetary Fund (IMF), 19/295, December 2019.

Claeys, G. and G.B. Wolff (2020), "Is the COVID-19 Crisis an Opportunity to Boost the Euro as a Global Currency?", *Policy Contribution*, Brugel, issue 11, June 5, 2020.

Committee on the Global Financial System (CGFS) (2020), "US Dollar Funding: An International Perspective", *CGFS Papers*, Bank for International Settlements (BIS), no.65, June 2020.

Davies, G. (2020), "The Safe-Asset Shortage after Covid-19", *Financial Times*, June 28, 2020.

Eichengreen, B. and D. Gros (2020), *Post-COVID-19 Global Currency Order: Risks and Opportunities for the Euro, Study for the Committee on Economic and Monetary Affairs, Policy Department for Economic, Scientific and Quality of Life Policies*, Luxembourg: European Parliament, September 2020.

Epstein, G. (2019), "The Asset Management Industry in the United States", *Financing for Development*, United Nations, no.271, December 2019.

European Central Bank (ECB) (2014), *Euro Repo Market: Improvement for Collateral and Liquidity Management*, European Central Bank (ECB), July 2014.

European Systemic Risk Board (ESRB) (2023), *EU Non-Bank Financial Intermediation Risk Monitor 2023*, European Systemic Risk Board (ESRB), June 6, 2023.

Fostel, A., J. Geanakoplos, and G. Phelan (2019), Global Collateral and Capital Flows, *NBER Working Paper Series*, National Bureau of Economic Research (NBER), no.25583, December 2019.

Gorton, G. and A. Metrick (2012a), "Securitized Banking and the Run on Repo", *Journal of Financial Economics*, vol.104, issue 3, June 2012, pp.425–451.

Gorton, G. and A. Metrick (2012b), "Securitization", *NBER Working Paper*, National Bureau of Economic Research (NBER), no.18611, December 2012.

Group of Thirty (2021), *US Treasury Markets: Steps Toward Increased Resilience*, Group of Thirty, July 2021.

Guse, M., W. Park, Z. Saravay, and Y. Yook (2019). "Collateralized Loan Obligations in the Financial Accounts of the United States", *FEDS Notes*, Board of Governors of the Federal Reserve System, September 20, 2019.

Hager, S.B. (2016), *Public Debt, Inequality and Power: The Making of a Modern Debt State*, Oakland: University of California Press.

Hager, S.B. (2017), "A Global Bond: Explaining the Safe-Haven Status of US Treasury Securities", *European Journal of International Relations*, vol.23, issue 3, 2017, pp.557–580.

Haldane, A.G. (2014), *The Age of Asset Management? Speech at the London Business School*, London, Bank of England (BOE), April 4, 2014.

He, Z., A. Krishnamurthy, and K. Milbradt (2016), "What Makes US Government Bonds Safe Assets?" *American Economic Review*, Papers & Proceedings 2016, vol.106, issue 5, pp.519–523.

Hempel, S., R.J. Kahn, R. Mann, and M. Paddrik (2024), "Repo Market Intermediation", *OFR Working Paper Series*, Office of Financial Research (OFR), 24-07, November 14, 2024.

Hung, H-F. (2016), *The China Boom: Why China Will Not Rule the World*, New York: Columbia University Press.

Infante, S., C. Press, and J. Strauss (2018), "The Ins and Outs of Collateral Re-use", *FEDS Notes*, Board of Governors of the Federal Reserve System, December 21, 2018.

Kahn, J.R. and L.M. Olson (2021), "Who Participates in Cleared Repo?", *OFR Working Paper*, Office of Financial Research (OFR), no.21-01, July 8, 2021.

Keller, J., C. Picillo, Z. Liu, J. Mazzacurati, P. Molitor, J. Söderberg, J. Theal, F. de Rossi, and R. Calleja (2014), "Securities Financing Transactions and the (Re) use of Collateral in Europe: An Analysis of the First Data Collection Conducted by the

ESRB from a Sample of European Banks and Agent Lenders", *ESRB Occasional Paper Series*, European Systemic Riks Board (ESRB), no.6, September 2014.

Kirschenmann, K., J. Riedler, and T. Schuler (2018), European Financial Integration through Securitization, *EconPol Policy Brief*, European Network of Economic and Fiscal Policy Research, November 2018.

Lannoo, K. and A. Thomadakis (2019), "Rebranding Capital Markets Union: A Market Finance Action Plan", *CEPS-ECMI Task Force Report*, Centre for European Policy Studies, June 2019.

Liu, E. and T. Schmidt-Eisenlohr (2019/2020). "Who Owns US CLO Securities?" *FEDS Notes*, Board of Governors of the Federal Reserve System, July 19, 2019 (Revised in June 25, 2020).

Mehrling, P. (2011), *The New Lombard Street: How the Fed Became the Dealer of Last Resort*, Princeton, NJ: Princeton University Press.

Murau, S., F. Pape, and T. Pforr (2022), "International Monetary Hierarchy through Emergency US-dollar Liquidity: A Key Currency Approach", *Competition & Change*, vol.27, issue 3–4, pp.495–515.

Paddrik, M.E., C.A. Ramírez, and M.J. McCormick (2021), "The Dynamics of the US Overnight Triparty Repo Market", *FEDS Notes*, Board of Governors of the Federal Reserve System, August 2, 2021.

Phillips, P. (2018), *Giants: The Global Power Elite*, New York: Seven Stories Press.

Ryan, P. and R. Toomey (2021), *Improving Capacity and Resiliency in US Treasury Markets: Part I*, Securities Industry and Financial Markets Association (SIFMA), March 24, 2021.

Schinasi, G.J., C.F. Kramer, and R.T. Smith (2001), "Financial Implications of the Shrinking Supply of U.S. Treasury Securities,' *IMF Working Paper*, International Monetary Fund (IMF), 01/61, May 2001.

Securities Industry and Financial Markets Association (SIFMA) (2022), US Repo Markets: A Chart Book, SIFMA Research, Securities Industry and Financial Markets Association (SIFMA), February 7, 2022.

Singh, M. (2011), "Velocity of Pledged Collateral: Analysis and Implications", *IMF Working Paper*, International Monetary Fund (IMF), 11/256, November 2011.

Singh, M. (2020), *Collateral Markets and Financial Plumbing*, Third Edition, London: Risk Books.

Tooze, A. (2018/2019), *Crashed: How a Decade of Financial Crises Changed the World*, London: Penguin Books.

US Department of the Treasury, Board of Governors of the Federal Reserve System, Federal Reserve Bank of New York, US Securities and Exchange Commission, and US Commodity Futures Trading Commission (2015), *Joint Staff Report: The US Treasury Market on October 15, 2014*, July 13, 2015.

Wu, S. and H. Nabilou (2018), "Repo Markets across the Atlantic: Similar but Unalike", *European Business Law Review*, vol.30, issue 4, pp.513–546.

7 The US dollar standard system at a watershed

1 The structural imbalances for US Treasury market intermediation since the GFC

As discussed in Chapter 6, US Treasury securities act as universal collateral assets for the endogenous finance of the global dollar in the shadow banking system, which helped global systemically important banks (G-SIBs) expand their gross balance sheets in the dollar in the 2010s. In other words, due to the predominant role of US Treasuries as universal collateral assets, the dysfunction in US Treasury market intermediation might contribute to building up global financial fragility that triggers global financial stress or panic in certain cases.

Traditionally, dealer banks, central subsidiaries of G-SIBs, have played an essential role in intermediation in US Treasury markets. Dealer's intermediation using their own balance sheets in the Treasury markets allows market participants worldwide to quickly purchase or sell US Treasuries in all market conditions without causing a drastic change in the securities' prices, thus contributing to market liquidity in the Treasury markets.[1] Notably, dealer banks underwent structural changes in their gross balance sheet activities for intermediation in US Treasury markets in the 2010s, which have two features. First, dealer banks switched their market-making activities in the Treasury markets from the matched book model, where dealer banks use their own gross balance sheets to accommodate client trading demands, to an order-driven model and/or brokerage model where they primarily match clients wishing to trade in opposite directions.[2] Second, the post-crisis changes in regulatory frameworks for G-SIBs lowered the capacity of dealer banks to use their gross balance sheets for US Treasury market intermediation. Since the Global Financial Crisis (GFC) of 2007–09, financial reforms including Base III and the Dodd-Frank Act were made to strengthen the resilience of the banking sector. US regulators adopted the supplementary leverage ratio (SLR), which was established in 2014 as part of the Basel III reforms, for large bank holding companies. While banks are subject to specific Federal Reserve prudential standards and must maintain an SLR of at least 3 percent, the

DOI: 10.4324/9781003733959-11

eight US G-SIBs are subject to the enhanced SLR, which effectively requires them to maintain an SLR of at least 5 percent (Tapia, Leung and Hamandi 2024). This has motivated larger banks and dealer banks to limit using their gross balance sheets dedicated for low-margin businesses such as Treasury market intermediation.[3]

The pullback of dealer banks from using their gross balance sheets for US Treasury market intermediation has increasingly moved the supply of market liquidity for US Treasury markets outside of dealers, in favor of a broader set of nonbank financial institutions (NBFIs). Two types of NBFIs stood out in US Treasury market intermediation in the 2010s: principal trade firms (PTFs) and hedge funds.[4] First, PTFs, which are more lightly regulated and hold relatively limited capital on their own account, emerged as major suppliers of market liquidity in US Treasury markets.[5] PTFs grow their presence in the rising electronic trading platforms called 'Electronification' (Markets Committee 2016) which enable automated trading (AT) to become prevalent in US Treasury market intermediation. An important form of AT in the Treasury markets is high-frequency trading (HFT). Over 50 percent of trading volumes in US Treasury securities were conducted through HFT.[6] Second, hedge funds are also major suppliers of market liquidity through 'the cash-future basis trade' in US Treasury markets since 2018, in which they sought to arbitrage profits by taking short positions in the Treasury futures and long positions in the Treasury cash. US Treasuries exposures of large hedge funds doubled from early 2018 to February 2020, reaching $1.45 trillion and $0.94 trillion in long and short exposure, respectively (Banegas, Monin and Petrasek 2021). According to a sample of trading activity shares for all securities by participant type from August 1, 2017, to July 31, 2018, while dealer banks still intermediate around half of the activity in all US Treasury securities (51 percent), PTFs and the buy-side investors such as hedge funds accounted for 21 percent and 28 percent, respectively (Brainard 2018). Hence, dealer banks retreated from their US Treasury market intermediation in the 2010s, as the position of NBFIs such as PTFs and hedge funds rose significantly.

With the structural pullback of dealer banks from US Treasury market intermediation in the 2010s, the question of whether or not dealers' intermediation for the Treasury markets contributes fully to supplying market liquidity becomes even more important, as the volume of the Treasury markets continues to grow dramatically in the decade. Growing US federal deficits since the GFC of 2007–09 caused the stock of marketable US Treasury securities to significantly grow, in comparison with the structural reduction in the aggregate size of dealer bankers' assets in the US since then (Burne 2021). As illustrated in Figure 7.1, in the second quarter of 2007 just before the GFC, the outstanding total financial assets at dealer banks ($6,545.1 billion) exceeded the outstanding of marketable US Treasury securities ($4,294.5 billion). In this sense, dealer banks had capacity for US Treasury market intermediation in the 2000s before the GFC.

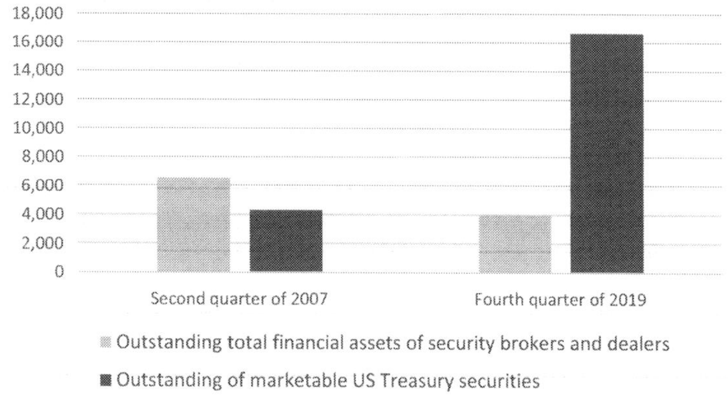

Figure 7.1 Structural Imbalance between Dealer Bank's Assets and the Outstanding US Treasury Securities ($ Billion)

Source: Board of Governors of the Federal Reserve System, Flow of funds of the United States.

However, the stock of marketable US Treasury bonds soared drastically in the 2010s, which substantially surpassed the outstanding total financial assets at dealer banks. While the outstanding total financial assets at dealer banks fell by 39.7 percent, decreasing from $6,545.1 billion in the second quarter of 2007 to $3,944.8 in the fourth quarter of 2019, the stock of marketable US Treasury securities increased by 287.2 percent, rising from $4,294.5 billion to $16.628.9 billion, respectively (Figure 7.1). As a result, the volume of marketable US Treasury securities was more than four times the total of financial assets at dealer banks as of the fourth quarter of 2019 just prior to the outbreak of the COVID-19 financial turmoil in March 2020.

The sizable imbalances between the reduction of dealer banks' capacity for US Treasury market intermediation and the culminative outstanding US Treasury bonds pointed to a potential dysfunctionality in the supply of market liquidity in US Treasury markets, if the Treasury markets were vulnerable to acute stress and shock. Such a possible dysfunctionality has, in effect, emerged as greater frequency of market illiquidity in the Treasury markets, where available market liquidity dried up very quickly in the 'taper tantrum' in 2013,[7] the 'flash rally' of October 15, 2014,[8] and the distress in US repo markets in September 2019,[9] although each stress in the Treasury markets differed in their scope and magnitude. In the stress event of US repo markets in September 2019, repo rates jumped from approximately 200 basis points to nearly 1,000 basis points in two days. Combined with the unwinding in the Fed's Quantitative Easing (QE), the structural reduction in dealer banks' intermediation capacity in the Treasury markets no longer allowed dealers to intermediate US Treasury securities when they reached the limit of their inventories to absorb the substantial sales of US Treasury bonds (Ryan and Toomey 2021).

In short, the structural constraints in dealer banks' capacity for US Treasury market intermediation, compared to the substantial sales of US Treasuries, contributed to dealer banks building up financial fragility that triggered the recurrent market illiquidity in the US Treasury markets in the 2010s.

2 The COVID-19 financial meltdown in US Treasury markets in March 2020

Following the recurrence of market illiquidity in US Treasury markets in the 2010s, the outbreak of the COVID-19 pandemic perpetuated a 'global dash for cash', driving a broad range of market participants worldwide to significantly sell large amounts of US Treasury securities perceived as 'risky', or not 'safe' in March 2020.[10]

First, US domestic investors including hedge funds and mutual funds unloaded US Treasury securities.[11] As previously explained, hedge funds pursued the cash-future basis trade in US Treasury markets to seek arbitrage differences in market prices between the value of futures and the cash in the Treasury markets since 2018. But, as the spike in the global dash for cash in the Treasury markets brought about a decoupling in the cash price of US Treasuries relative to futures, the arbitrage trade became loss-making. This led to a large-scale unwinding of the cash-future basis trade by hedge funds, which reduced their holdings of US Treasuries by $127 billion in March (Banegas, Monin and Petrasek 2021). Second, mutual funds sold US Treasury securities in exceptionally large volumes, as these funds monetized their most liquid assets (i.e., US Treasuries) to raise cash to meet investors' redemptions and rebalance their portfolios. Net sales of US Treasury bonds by US domestic mutual funds were estimated to be $266 billion in the first quarter of 2020, or 20 percent of their holdings at the end of 2019 (Banegas, Monin and Petrasek 2021).

In response to the massive sales of US Treasury bonds by US domestic investors, could foreign investors, especially foreign central banks, purchase large amounts of significantly US Treasury securities like the GFC of 2007–09? In contrast to the GFC period, foreign investors were significant sellers in the US Treasury markets with $417 billion in net sales in March 2020 (Weiss 2022), which largely reflected foreign central banks in emerging market economies raising dollar cash to meet the dollar shortage of non-US banks or to intervene in foreign exchange markets. Figure 7.2 compares net purchases of US Treasury securities (as a percentage of pre-crisis holdings) by major emerging markets economies across the two crises: the Global Financial Crisis and the COVID-19 financial turmoil.

The top ten emerging market economies became 'net sellers' with $240 billion of US Treasury securities on the eve of the COVID-19 financial

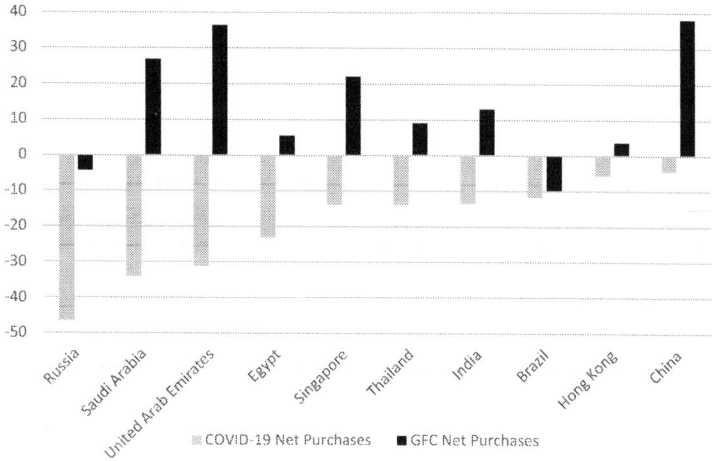

Figure 7.2 Major Emerging Market Economies Sellers of US Treasury Securities in the GFC Period and the COVID-19 Pandemic Period ($ Billion)

Source: Reproduced from Weiss (2022), Figure 2.

Notes: The data show percent of pre-crisis holdings. GFC months are September–November 2008; COVID-19 months are March and April 2020. While the figure includes net purchases by both foreign private and foreign official investors, the vast majority of these net purchases are likely by foreign official investors.

turbulence, compared to their 'net purchases' of US Treasuries at the height of the GFC (Weiss 2022). In short, the unusual sell-off of US Treasury securities triggered an inconsistency in the powerful bond of interest between US domestic and foreign owners for US Treasury bonds at the height of the COVID-19 financial turmoil.

Amid the inconsistency in the powerful bond of interest between US domestic and foreign owners for US Treasuries, were there other middlemen buying US Treasuries being sold off during the financial distress? The answer is 'no'. First, NBFIs such as PTFs could not absorb the extraordinary selling of US Treasury securities during this time of financial stress. Second, most importantly, dealer banks' capacity for using their gross balance sheets for Treasury market intermediation was inelastic at the outset of the COVID-19 financial turmoil.[12] The extremely massive sales in US Treasury markets at the height of the COVID-19 financial distress quickly began to overwhelm the dealer banks' capacity for absorbing the substantial selling of US Treasury securities, as recognized in the quotation from the US Fed's Financial Stability Report in May 2020:

> Dealer intermediation in the Treasury market received considerable attention during the intense market volatility in March. As investors sold

> less-liquid Treasury securities to obtain cash, dealers absorbed large amounts of these Treasury securities onto their balance sheets. It is possible that some dealers reached their capacity to absorb these sales, leading to a deterioration in Treasury market functioning.
>
> (Board of Governors of the Federal Reserve System (2020, p.29) (Underline is by author)

Indeed, dealers' gross bond inventories and daily purchases of bonds from customers surged to over ten times their 2017–22 medians in US Treasury markets (Duffie 2023). As a result, dealer banks essentially ran out of their gross balance sheet capacity to absorb the massive sales of US Treasuries in March 2020. This substantial lack of dealers' capacity for US Treasury market intermediation, in turn, boosted market illiquidity in the Treasury markets. Bid-ask spreads, one measure of market liquidity, for the on-the-run 30-year bond widened to more than six times the post-Global Financial Crisis average by mid-March 2020.[13] Looking historically at US Treasury markets, the scale and scope of the COVID-19 financial meltdown is the first time since the collapse of the Bretton Woods (BW) system in the early 1970s that its market liquidity condition became extremely deteriorated.[14]

Thus, the extraordinary selling of US Treasury securities in the face of the COVID-19 financial turmoil contributed to dealer banks, central subsidiaries of G-SIBs, lacking capacity for US Treasury market intermediation using their gross balance sheets, leading to the first market illiquidity in the Treasury markets at this scale and scope since the advent of the dollar standard system in the early 1970s.

3 The dysfunctionality in US Treasury securities as universal collateral assets

As previously noted, in the face of the GFC of 2007–09, the powerful bond of interest between US domestic and foreign owners of US public debts shored up the structural demand for US Treasury securities, which contributed to nourishing market liquidity in US Treasury markets in the 2010s. By contrast, the inconsistency in the formidable bond of interest between US domestic and foreign owners for US Treasury bonds led to the extraordinary sell-off of US Treasuries at the height of the COVID-19 financial turmoil in March 2020, which boosted the market illiquidity in US Treasury markets. Tooze (2021) describes below how the market illiquidity in the Treasury markets (the largest, deepest, most liquidity financial markets in the world) in March 2020 would have destabilized the global financial system more than GFC of 2007–09:

> At the top of the pyramid of safe assets are dollar-denominated US Treasuries...On March 13 (2020: author), JP Morgan reported that rather than a normal market depth of hundreds of millions of dollars in US Treasuries, it

> was possible to trade no more than $12 million without noticeably moving the price. That was less than one-tenth of normal market liquidity. This was a state of financial panic, which if it had been allowed to develop, would have been more destabilizing even than the failure of Lehman Brothers in September 2008.
>
> (pp.111–112; underlines are by author)

What impact did the market illiquidity in Treasury markets as the largest, deepest, and most liquid financial markets in the world have on the endogenous finance of the global dollar in the shadow banking system, which helped G-SIBs' gross balance sheets denominated in the dollar?

Crucially, the market illiquidity in US Treasury markets during COVID-19 financial distress made US Treasury securities as safest assets dysfunctional. Given this dysfunctionality, G-SIBs including dealer banks could no longer use US Treasuries as universal collateral assets, by which an unprecedented pressure of the endogenous finance of the global dollar in the shadow banking system emerged at the height of the COVID-19 financial meltdown.[15] The destructive nature of the global dollar supply would, ceteris paribus, have resulted in the collapse of USD-denominated gross balance sheets at G-SIBs that could have destabilized the dollar standard system.[16]

Accordingly, the dysfunctionality in US Treasury securities as universal collateral assets offers a suggestion that the COVID-19 financial meltdown in March 2020 caused marked the US dollar standard system to undergo a kind of watershed in the 2010s.

Notes

1 The dealer bank intermediation for US Treasury securities markets is divided into three trades: dealer-to-client (DTC), dealer-to-dealer (DTD), and interdealer broker (IDB). TMPG (2022) provides a detailed explanation of clearing and settlement in US Treasury markets through dealers' intermediation.

2 CGFS (2014, 2016); FSB (2020); Liang and Parkinson (2020); Aramonte, Schrimpf and Shin (2021/2022); US Department of the Treasury, Board of Governors of the Federal Reserve System, Federal Reserve Bank of New York, US Securities and Exchange Commission, and US Commodity Futures Trading Commission (2021); Group of Thirty (2021); Scheicher and Schrimpf (2022).

3 US Department of the Treasury, Board of Governors of the Federal Reserve System, Federal Reserve Bank of New York, US Securities and Exchange Commission, and US Commodity Futures Trading Commission (2021), p.5.

4 Also, US domestic institutional investors including money market funds (MMFs) became a major supplier of market liquidity in US Treasury markets. One important reason is that the 2014 Securities and Exchange Commission (SEC) reform of the money market fund (MMF) required the affected MMFs to price their shares at floating net asset value, rather than the traditional $1 per share.

5 Though dealer banks and PTFs compete when it comes to market liquidity provision in the Treasury markets, there is still a relationship that dealer banks usually act as a prime brokering for PTFs (Aramonte, Schrimpf and Shin [2021/2022], p.8).

6 US Department of the Treasury, Board of Governors of the Federal Reserve System, Federal Reserve Bank of New York, US Securities and Exchange Commission, and US Commodity Futures Trading Commission (2021), p.51.
7 Adrian et al. (2013).
8 US Department of the Treasury, Board of Governors of the Federal Reserve System, Federal Reserve Bank of New York, US Securities and Exchange Commission, and US Commodity Futures Trading Commission (2015); Bouveret et al. (2015).
9 Afonso et al. (2021); Ryan and Toomey (2021); Paddrik et al. (2023).
10 Cheng, Wessel and Younger (2020); Duffie (2020, 2023); FSB (2020); He and Krishnamurthy (2020); Liang and Parkinson (2020); Logan (2020); Group of Thirty (2021).
11 In addition, US household sector was also net seller of $152 billion in the first quarter of 2020 (Banegas, Monin and Petrasek 2021).
12 For example, Duffie (2020).
13 US Department of the Treasury, Board of Governors of the Federal Reserve System, Federal Reserve Bank of New York, US Securities and Exchange Commission, and US Commodity Futures Trading Commission (2021), p.12.
14 The COVID-19 financial meltdown is the fourth time that the Treasury markets became extremely dysfunctional after the first three, in 1939, 1958, and 1970 since the 20th century (Garbade 2021).
15 Eriksson von Allmen et al. (2020) note that a pressure of global dollar funding emerged in unprecedented magnitude in the face of the COVID-19 financial turmoil in March 2020.
16 The market liquidity condition in the US Treasury markets restored quickly since the COVID-19 financial meltdown in March 2020. One of the main factors is that the US Fed acts as 'the buyer of last resort' in US Treasury markets (Kindleberger, Aliber and McCauley 1978/2023, p.331) where there were, in effect, no buyers on the eve of the COVID-19 financial distress. As a result, the Fed purchased nearly $1 trillion of US Treasury bonds within the three-week period beginning March 16, 2020 (Group of Thirty 2021, p.3). Another main factor is the extension in the Fed role as international lender of last resort (LLR) beyond the global swap network established during the GFC, which was divided into two features. First, the Fed extended the swap network lines with major central banks more broadly, including central banks in emerging market countries. Second, more importantly, the Fed set in motion foreign and international monetary authorities (FIMA) repo facility to minimize for foreign central banks to sell significantly US Treasury securities at the end of March 2020. The FIMA allows non-US central banks facing dollar shortages to pledge US Treasury bonds as collateral assets with the Fed for borrowing USD-denominated central bank deposits. On July 2021, the FIMA repo facility was finally made permanent (Murau, Pape and Pforr [2022], pp.8–12). Nevertheless, the level of market liquidity in US Treasury markets still remains low in the 2020s. Market depth, one measure of market liquidity, in the Treasury markets has been steadily improving since hitting its lows in early 2022, but remains about 50 percent below its decade-long average (JP Morgan [2024], p.3).

References

Adrian, T., M.J. Fleming, J.E. Goldberg, M. Lewis, F.M. Natalucci, and J.J. Wu (2013), "Dealer Balance Sheet Capacity and Market Liquidity during the 2013 Selloff in Fixed-Income Markets", *Liberty Street Economics*, Federal Reserve Bank of New York, October 16, 2013.

Afonso, G., M. Cipriani, A. Copeland, A. Kovner, G.L. Spada, and A. Martin (2021), "The Market Events of Mid-September 2019", Economic Policy Review, Federal Reserve Bank of New York, vol.27, issue 2, pp.1–24.

Aramonte, S., A. Schrimpf, and H.S. Shin (2021/2022), "Non-Bank Financial Intermediaries and Financial Stability", *BIS Working Papers*, Bank for International Settlements (BIS), no.972, October 2021 (Revised in January 2022).

Banegas, A., P.J. Monin, and L. Petrasek (2021), "Sizing Hedge Funds' Treasury Market Activities and Holdings", *FEDS Notes*, Board of Governors of the Federal Reserve System, October 6, 2021.

Board of Governors of the Federal Reserve System (2020), *Financial Stability Report*, Board of Governors of the Federal Reserve System, May 2020.

Bouveret, A., P. Breuer, Y. Chen, D. Jones, and T. Sasaki (2015), "Fragilities in the US Treasury Market: Lessons from the "Flash Rally" of October 15, 2014", *IMF Working Paper*, International Monetary Fund (IMF), 15/222, October 2015.

Brainard, L. (2018): "The Structure of the Treasury Market: What Are We learning?", *Speech at the FRBNY Annual Conference on the Evolving Structure of the US Treasury Market*, Federal Reserve Bank of New York, December 3, 2018.

Burne, K. (2021), "Future-Proofing the US Treasury Market", *Aerial View*, Bank of New York Mellon, November 16, 2021.

Cheng, J., D. Wessel, and J. Younger (2020), *How did COVID-19 Disrupt the Market for US Treasury Debt? The Hutchins Center on Fiscal and Monetary Policy*, Brookings Institution, May 1, 2020.

Committee on the Global Financial System (CGFS) (2014), "Market-Making and Proprietary Trading: Industry Trends, Drivers and Policy Implications", *CGFS Papers*, Bank for International Settlements (BIS), no.52, November 2014.

Committee on the Global Financial System (CGFS) (2016), "Fixed Income Market Liquidity", *CGFS Papers*, Bank for International Settlements (BIS), no.55, January 2016.

Duffie, D. (2020), "Still the World's Safe Haven? Redesigning the US Treasury Market after the COVID-19 Crisis", *Hutchins Center Working Paper*, Brookings Institution, no.62, June 2020.

Duffie, D. (2023), "Resilience Redux in the US Treasury Market", *Jackson Hole Symposium*, Federal Reserve Bank of Kansas City, September 2, 2023.

Eriksson von Allmen, U., P. Jeasakul, H. Kang, and P. Khera (2020), "Macrofinancial Considerations for Assessing the Impact of the COVID-19 Pandemic", *Special Series on COVID-19*, International Monetary Fund (IMF), May 6, 2020.

Financial Stability Board (FSB) (2020), *Holistic Review of the March Market Turmoil*, Financial Stability Board (FSB), November 17, 2020.

Garbade, K. (2021), *After the Accord: A History of Federal Reserve Open Market Operations, the US Government Securities Market, and Treasury Debt Management from 1951 to 1979*, Cambridge: Cambridge University Press.

Group of Thirty (2021), *US Treasury Markets: Steps toward Increased Resilience*, Group of Thirty, July 2021.

He, Z. and A. Krishnamurthy (2020), Are US Treasury Bonds Still a Safe Haven? *The Reporter*, National Bureau of Economic Research (NBER), no.3, October 2020.

JP Morgan (2024), *This One's Optimistic: Broad Improvements in Treasury Market Liquidity Trends in 2024, North America Fixed Income Strategy*, JP Morgan, June 21, 2024.

Kindleberger, C.P., R.Z. Aliber, and R.N. McCauley (1978/2023), *Manias, Panics, and Crashes: A History of Financial Crises,* Eighth Edition, Cham: Palgrave Macmillan.

Liang, N. and P. Parkinson (2020), "Enhancing Liquidity of the US Treasury Market under Stress", *Hutchins Center Working Papers*, Brookings Institution, no.72, December 2020.

Logan, L.K. (2020), Treasury Market Liquidity and Early Lessons from the Pandemic Shock, *Remarks at Brookings-Chicago Booth Task Force on Financial Stability (TFFS) Meeting*, Panel on Market Liquidity, Federal Reserve Bank of New York, October 23, 2020.

Murau, S., F. Pape, and T. Pforr (2022), "International Monetary Hierarchy through Emergency US-dollar Liquidity: A Key Currency Approach", *Competition & Change*, vol.27, issue 3–4, pp.495–515.

Paddrik, M., H.P. Young, R.J. Kahn, M. McCormick, and V. Nguyen (2023), "Anatomy of the Repo Rate Spikes in September 2019", *OFR Working Paper*, Office of Financial Research (OFR), 23-04, April 25, 2023.

Ryan, P. and R. Toomey (2021), Improving Capacity and Resiliency in US Treasury Markets: Part I, Securities Industry and Financial Markets Association (SIFMA), March 24, 2021.

Scheicher, M. and A. Schrimpf (2022), "Liquidity in Bond Markets-Navigating in Troubled Waters", *SUERF Policy Brief*, European Money and Financial Forum, no.395, August 2022.

Tapia, J.M., R. Leung, and H. Hamandi (2024), Banks' Supplementary Leverage Ratio, *The OFR Blog*, Office of Financial Research (OFR), August 2, 2024.

The Treasury Market Practices Group (TMPG) (2022), White Paper on Clearing and Settlement in the Market for US Treasury Secured Financing Transactions, Federal Reserve Bank of New York, November 9, 2022.

Tooze, A. (2021), *Shutdown: How Covid Shook the World's Economy*, New York: Viking.

US Department of the Treasury, Board of Governors of the Federal Reserve System, Federal Reserve Bank of New York, US Securities and Exchange Commission, and US Commodity Futures Trading Commission (2015), *Joint Staff Report: The US Treasury Market on October 15, 2014*, July 13, 2015.

US Department of the Treasury, Board of Governors of the Federal Reserve System, Federal Reserve Bank of New York, US Securities and Exchange Commission, and US Commodity Futures Trading Commission (2021), *Recent Disruptions and Potential Reforms in the US Treasury Market: A Staff Progress Report*, November 8, 2021.

Weiss, C.R. (2022), "Foreign Demand for US Treasury Securities during the Pandemic", *FEDS Notes*, Board of Governors of the Federal Reserve System, January 28, 2022.

8 Conclusion

This book presents novel arguments for understanding the fundamentals, nature, and present structure of the US dollar standard system since the 2000s, by focusing on the endogenous finance of the global dollar backed by US debt securities, especially US Treasury securities, as collateral assets in the shadow banking system, which contributes to the dynamic process of USD-denominated gross balance sheets at global systemically important banks (G-SIBs). Our arguments provide three contributions for discussion on the contemporary dollar standard system, in contrast to the main features of the money view which has for several years become increasingly common among heterodox economists.

First, the comparative advantage of the US shadow banking system interlinking with offshore financial centers (OFCs) over the one in the Eurozone encouraged G-SIBs to denominate their gross balance sheets in the dollar, rather than the euro, in the 2000s. The money view takes the US dollar standard system for granted, in the sense that the international monetary system is inherently viewed as a hierarchical system where the dollar has been dominant and then other major currencies have been pushed down to peripheral positions.

But it is incorrect that the US dollar's staying power has always been unrivaled. The dollar's dominance has, gradually but distinctly, been undermined by the internationalization of the German Deutsche mark and Japanese yen since the second half of the 1980s, and then the rising role of the euro in the 2000s. The emergence of the euro was the first time since the collapse of the Bretton Woods (BW) system that the US dollar standard system faced real currency competition in the 2000s. What enabled the dollar to revive its dominance in the 2000s, despite the currency competition with the euro?

Recall our discussion that the comparative advantage of the US shadow banking system compared to the less developed shadow banking system of the Eurozone determined G-SIBs to denominate their gross balance sheets in the dollar, despite the emergence of the euro in the 2000s. This, in turn, led to strong demand for USD-denominated long-term privately debt securities (e.g., MBSs, ABSs, and CDOs) and short-term liquid financial instruments

DOI: 10.4324/9781003733959-12

(e.g., repos, ABCPs, and FX swaps) created by G-SIBs in the shadow banking system. As such, the dollar's dominance in the shadow banking system enabled the dollar to revive its dominance in the 2000s prior to the Global Financial Crisis (GFC) of 2007–09.

Accordingly, regarding the fundamentals of the US dollar standard system in the 2000s, it is proposed that the dollar standard system should not be taken for granted as the money view emphasizes, but is the dynamic outcome of the currency competition in the shadow banking system between the dollar and the euro in the 2000s.

Second, the endogenous finance of the global dollar in the shadow banking system is, by its nature, more elastic and leveraged than that of the traditional banking system, which enabled G-SIBs to expand USD-denominated gross balance sheets in the 2000s prior to the GFC. The money view insists that the evolution in the hierarchical structure of the global dollar supply contributes to the US dollar standard having an essentially systemic nature.

However, the dollar standard system has essentially entailed global financial instability. Looking historically at the US dollar standard system since the 1970s, we can see that the unfettered global capital flows have triggered the recurrence of international currency and monetary crises around the globe that climaxed with the GFC of 2007–09, which had its very epicenter in the US. What drove the dollar standard system to contribute to the buildup of global financial fragility in the 2000s that led to the GFC?

Remember our argument that the endogenously elastic supply of the global dollar in the shadow banking system contributed to the buildup of global financial fragility in the 2000s, leading to the GFC of 2007–09. Particular emphasis is placed on the dynamics in global collateral plumbing, combined with the procyclical mechanism in USD-denominated gross balance sheets at G-SIBs, accelerating the endogenous financing of the global dollar to become highly elastic in the shadow banking system during the US housing bubble (2004–06). The endogenously highly elastic finance of the global dollar in the shadow banking system contributed to the overstretched nature of USD-denominated gross balance sheets at G-SIBs that climaxed in the GFC.

Therefore, with respect to the nature of the US dollar standard system in the 2000s, it is reasonable to suppose that the US dollar standard system centered around the shadow banking had a dynamic and ultimately destructive nature that culminated in the GFC, in contrary to the money view's assumption that the dollar standard has an essentially systemic nature.

Third, US Treasury securities serve as universal collateral assets for the endogenous finance of the global dollar in the shadow banking system, which helped G-SIBs expand their gross balance sheets denominated in the dollar in the 2010s. The money view suggests that the evolution in the US Fed's role as international lender of last resort (LLR) since the GFC of 2007–09 contributes to the status quo dollar standard where the dollar remains at the apex in the 2010s.

Nevertheless, the extraordinary sell-off in the US Treasury markets as the largest, deepest, and most liquid financial markets in the world at the height of the COVID-19 financial meltdown in March 2020 would have destabilized the dollar standard system even more than the GFC, if it had been allowed to develop. What caused the massive selling in US Treasury markets, leading to the unprecedented global dollar funding pressures, though a global financial crisis was averted?

Recall our debate that the unusually high sales in the US Treasury markets in the face of the COVID-19 financial distress led to the US Treasury markets facing the first market illiquidity in its scale and scope since the advent of the dollar standard system in the early 1970s, which made US Treasury securities as safest assets dysfunctional. Given this dysfunctionality, G-SIBs including dealer banks could no longer use US Treasuries as universal collateral assets, by which an unprecedented pressure of the endogenous finance of the global dollar in the shadow banking system emerged at the height of the COVID-19 financial turmoil. The destructive nature of the global dollar supply would, *ceteris paribus*, have resulted in the collapse of USD-denominated gross balance sheets at G-SIBs that could have destabilized the dollar standard system even more than the GFC of 2007–09.

Consequently, with regard to the present structure of the US dollar standard system in the 2010s, it is possible that the US dollar standard system centered around the shadow banking underwent a kind of watershed, characterized by the dysfunctionality in US Treasury securities as universal collateral assets at the height of the COVID-19 financial meltdown; in contrast, the money view conjectures that the evolution in the Fed's role as international LLR since the GFC contributes to status quo dollar standard where the dollar remains dominant in the 2010s.

All in all, taking account of our arguments of the fundamentals, nature, and present structure of the dollar standard system since the 2000s, the contemporary dollar standard system has developed around shadow banking since the 2000s but has also proven dynamic and ultimately destructive in the face of the GFC of 2007–09, and the COVID-19 financial meltdown in US Treasury markets in March 2020 marks that the dollar standard underwent a kind of watershed. Particular importance in our discussions is placed on the unparalleled status of US debt securities, especially US Treasury securities, as collateral assets, determining the fundamentals, nature, and present structure of the dollar standard system since the 2000s, which is typically overlooked or dismissed as irrelevant in the money view.

What will the unrivaled position of US Treasury securities as universal collateral assets look like in the foreseeable future? In order to answer this question, further study should be conducted on how market-driven demand for US Treasuries as collateral assets in shadow banking system, which we have argued in the book, and foreign official demand for them are fundamentally linked (Tokunaga 2019). In other words, we need to capture how the market value and creditworthiness of US Treasury securities as collateral assets will ultimately be sustained by foreign official holdings of US Treasuries in the foreseeable future. In doing so, it is necessary to integrate the US's dominance in the political and geopolitical realm into our argument that the dollar standard system developed around shadow banking. Foreign official demand for US Treasury bonds cannot be detached from the US's strong geopolitical and military relation to its allies. Over the past ten years, considering countries with any form of military link cooperation with the US as allies, around three-quarters of safe US assets held by foreign governments are held by allies (Weiss 2022). Such a discussion would undoubtedly contribute to exploring the foreseeable future of the dollar standard system.

References

Tokunaga, J. (2019), "The Revised US Treasury Securities Standard System", *PERI Working Paper*, Political Economy Research Institute (PERI), University of Massachusetts Amherst, no.494, September 2019.

Weiss, C. (2022), "Geopolitics and the US Dollar's Future as a Reserve Currency", *International Finance Discussion Papers*, Board of Governors of the Federal Reserve System, no.1359, October 2022.

Index

Note: *Italic* page numbers refer to figures and page numbers followed by "n" denote endnotes.

Made in the USA
Las Vegas, NV
19 September 2026

676aa6ee-6c1e-4ab9-bc4c-ee5821dc2a9fR01